HOW PEOPLE TICK

HOW PEOPLE TICK

A guide to over 50 types of difficult people and how to handle them

2nd edition

MIKE LEIBLING

KOGAN PAGE

London and Philadelphia

First published in Great Britain and the United States in 2005 by Kogan Page Limited
Reprinted in 2005, 2006, 2007
Second edition 2009

120 Pentonville Road	525 South 4th Street, #241
London N1 9JN	Philadelphia PA 19147
United Kingdom	USA
www.koganpage.com	

© Mike Leibling, 2005, 2009

The right of Mike Leibling to be identified as the author of this work has been asserted by him in accordance with the Copyright, Designs and Patents Act 1988.

ISBN 978 0 7494 5459 3

British Library Cataloguing-in-Publication Data

A CIP record for this book is available from the British Library.

Library of Congress Cataloging-in-Publication Data

Leibling, Mike.
  How people tick : a guide to over 50 types of difficult people and how to handle them / Mike Leibling. -- 2nd ed.
    p. cm.
  ISBN 978-0-7494-5459-3
  1. Interpersonal conflict. 2. Conflict management. I. Title.
  BF637.I48L55 2009
  158.2--dc22
                              2008054358

Typeset by Jean Cussons Typesetting, Diss, Norfolk
Printed and bound in India by Replika Press Pvt Ltd

Contents

About the author

Mike Leibling is a coach (with individuals) and trainer and facilitator (with groups and teams and boards) in the area of How to Get On With People You Don't Get On With (!).

He worked for nearly 20 years as a strategist with Saatchi & Saatchi, ultimately as International Strategic Planning Director. He had many clients, large and small, private, public and third sectors, and was increasingly called upon to spend his time doing training and coaching and mentoring.

Then in 1995 he founded Strategy Strategy™ to help people and organizations to move on in 'difficult' situations or, preferably, to spot them coming and so avoid them in the first place.

Preface to the second edition

This book is for everyone who finds people fascinating, bewildering or infuriating, and yet still wants to understand them, work with them and live with them.

Thanks to everyone for their feedback on the first edition – which ranged from 'My most difficult client has turned into a pussycat' to 'You've obviously met my mother-in-law as she's got a whole chapter to herself!'

The most common feedback, however, was 'Why haven't you written a chapter on X?' And so, dear readers, we now have *even more* difficult people that we can handle, right here at our fingertips:

- Disrespectful people   (pages 57–61)
- Gossipy people   (pages 78–77)
- Must-Have-The-Last-Word people   (pages 125–128)
- Plodders   (pages 143–145)
- Princesses(and princes   (pages 146–148)
- U-turners   (pages 196–199)

Thank you all.

Mike Leibling@StrategyStrategy.com
www.StrategyStrategy.com

Introduction

This book is about understanding patterns of behaviour that annoy us and how we can change them.

We often talk about difficult people, labelling an entire person as 'difficult' when in truth it may just be one aspect of their behaviour that we have found challenging. That's why this book explores exactly how people 'do' difficult, instead of 'are' difficult.

I dislike ideas such as *stress management*, because what is much more productive is stress *avoidance*. If we simply invest a little time in preventing a situation going wrong, we don't have to pick up the pieces afterwards.

But, over the years, I've noticed how people create stress by winding each other up time and time again, usually without wanting to, and with uncomfortable results. And I've also recognized that surprisingly common patterns of behaviour occur time and time again with people who naturally have very different individual backgrounds.

That's why I've written this book, because it's much easier – and more effective – to identify and deal with behavioural *patterns*, rather than having to handle each difficult *event*, time and time again.

So please dip in and enjoy these tried and tested tips for handling 'difficult' people in 'difficult' situations, based on a real understanding of their behaviour.

Angry people

*who may also be Aggressive, Antagonistic,
Argumentative, Confrontational, Destructive,
Explosive, Hostile, Intimidating, Threatening,
Vicious or even Violent*

What ticks us off

All of us feel angry at times, but people 'do' angry in different ways. Sometimes anger is directed very precisely at us, or at what we've said or done. At other times it seems as though it has nothing to do with us, and we're receiving the full force of what might have been meant for someone else. It can also come in three temperatures: hot, cold and neutral.

How it can happen

Anger is felt by everyone. It's a chemical thing, with all sorts of exciting chemicals being triggered off – to aid our survival. When people explode with anger, they are responding externally in the same way as the chemicals are reacting internally – ie wildly!

But – and this might be hard to believe at first – anger only lasts about 20 seconds maximum. The chemicals, after 20 seconds or so, start to subside. So how come some people seem angry for hours or days or for ever? That's because they follow the chemicals with thoughts. Typically, they start thinking of what the consequences might have been. Or they remember other people and occasions that have 'made them feel like this'. Or, very commonly, they start plotting revenge! And – not surprisingly – all these thought patterns start producing their own chemicals, and the vicious (= angry) circle goes round and round all by itself.

Sometimes anger is directed appropriately at us, for what we said or did, whether or not we meant to. At other times it can seem directed at us, or indeed at the whole world, for no apparent reason. It's almost as though the person has no internal compartments for containing it, and it has spread within him or her, and comes whooshing out at any opportunity. (Or, with some people, it seems like every opportunity.)

Let's now examine the different temperatures.

Hot anger happens almost instantly, often without warning, and can be really threatening. Some people seem literally to explode, and come over as physically threatening and in-your-face. As they are so incensed, they can seem wildly out of control. They often get really personal with their insults, and it's sometimes hard to hear what they are actually saying through their heated activity.

Cold anger is very, very calculated. The chemicals have subsided, and in the ensuing calm, the brain plots its next steps: what it is going to do, and how it can make itself felt. It can, therefore, be genuinely chilling. The message is clear. Every single word is clear. And the intention to have the message heard is chillingly clear and deliberate, in a controlled, almost clinically cutting way. And – unlike hot anger, which is pretty instantaneous – cold anger can sometimes be plotted and prepared and lie dormant for a very, very long time indeed.

'Inactions speak louder than words'

I have a friend who always expresses her feelings and thoughts out loud, all the time. Her boss was the opposite – he sulked in silence. One day we were chatting about how she'd never been able to persuade her boss that she was upset, no matter how much she expressed her feelings. I suggested to her that instead of emoting *her* way (ie loudly), she tried emoting her boss's way (ie coolly). The next evening she rang me, excitedly of course. 'It worked brilliantly. My boss asked me first thing if I'd had a good weekend. Instead of telling him all about my problems, as I used to do (to which my boss used to say automatically "Good"), I just sort of grunted and mumbled "OK", avoiding eye contact. Five minutes later he came back with a silly query – obviously made up. I just grunted a short answer back. Another five minutes later he rushed back shouting, "What on earth is wrong – I've never seen you like this before?" It worked: I got through by using his language (cool), not mine (hot).'

Neutral anger may sound like a contradiction in terms; how can 'anger' come over as 'neutral'? Surely it needs *energy* – either searingly hot, or deliberately held back and cold? Well, neutral anger is also calculated, but it states the obvious so that the message is simple and clear – rather than reinforced with hot dramatics, or chilling effect.

People from the United States can be especially brilliant at this, and can 'do' angry in a very neutral way, eg by saying calmly and factually 'What you did made me feel very, very angry.' (And then they leave a potentially endless pause, having said and done all that they chose to do, thus handing the baton over to the other person to accept the responsibility to respond.)

Tips for handling angry people

Hot anger can seem to consume the person who's 'doing' it, and there's usually little point in saying anything until there's less heat. A key tip is not to take it personally, as you'll be so mortified inside that you'll withdraw into yourself and the person will think you're ignoring them! So, the main things that a hot-anger person needs are:

■ not to be ignored, as they'd feel they're not getting through to you, and so they'd have to increase their signals;
■ not to be patronized, such as being told to Calm Down; it doesn't work when you're Angered Up!
■ not to be outdone; if you start telling them how angry or upset you are about their approach, or anything else, it denies them their agenda and voice;
■ to be noticed; good eye contact is important, but soften your gaze and don't stare!
■ to be acknowledged as 'angry' on a personal level, then to have some help to move the situation forward, on an impersonal 'what exactly needs to happen next' level.

A good way of acknowledging someone who is angry is to respect their position by saying, for instance, 'You're right.' And then leave a jolly good long pause in place for them to consider this. If they don't hear you (and 'being' angry seems to divert all the energy away from the ears), simply repeat it: 'You're right.'

And whenever I've said this, it has pretty much always taken the wind out of their sails. Or, as one client said, 'It really took my sails out of the wind, thank you.' When I asked how, he said that he knew he was right, and now that I knew he was right, he couldn't 'do' angry any more.

Is this being untrue to myself, saying that the other person is right? Not at all – because I truly believe that they are right to feel whatever they feel. (I am not, however, saying that I would feel the same if I were in their shoes.)

'No, Mr Nicholls'

I was working in a shoe shop in Brighton, between leaving school and starting college. One Saturday, the tallest and second-angriest man I have ever seen came thundering into the shop, pulled me outside and pointed to the window display. 'I want that pair of shoes for my wife.' I assumed that the woman a few steps behind him was the wife in question and a quick glance at her feet suggested that the shoes in the window would be much too small. I explained that we put the smallest shoes in the window display, so we could fit more in. I explained that his wife's feet were not the same size as the shoes in question. I explained that the window dresser was not in attendance (yes, I think I actually used that phrase!) until Tuesday – and none of this worked. He pretty soon turned into the first-angriest man I'd ever seen. Eventually he stormed out of the shop, dragging a rather pale wife but leaving behind a stream of colourful language.

The manager, Mr Nicholls, came up to me, and in his kindly way hit the nail on the head when he gently said 'Well, Mr Leibling, I don't think you could have handled that much worse, could you?' He was absolutely right. I had tried everything except the tips above!

 TIP

Count to 10

Cold and neutral anger are highly effective in practice because they are the considered responses to a situation and internal chemical reactions that have already cooled down – so there's no external 'situation' to cool down to begin with. (The old suggestions of counting slowly to 10 before responding, or 'holding your tongue' or 'biting your lip', come to mind here.)

'Out of the mouths'

I remember being out for dinner with friends. Their three-year-old (who had previously been banished to his room for a minor misdemeanour) came slowly down the stairs. He calmly stopped halfway, paused, and then looked from parent to parent. He quietly said 'You make me very unhappy' and then, oh so slowly, turned back upstairs again – leaving the three of us with enormous lumps in our throats.

The principles, however, are exactly the same as for hot anger. For example, with the three-year-old child in the case study we might say something like 'You're right.' (Pause) 'I'm sorry I made you unhappy.' (Pause) 'Come here and tell me what you want me to do.' (Pause) 'And we'll have a big cuddle while I'm listening.' This:

■ acknowledges the person and their feelings;
■ acknowledges your own position;
■ makes it clear that you intend putting things right, by listening to their thoughts;
■ moves the situation forward by putting the event into the past tense, where it belongs; even though the child said, 'you make me very unhappy', we contain the event in the past tense.

Tips for handling angry people

Full stops

After you've said what you need to say, shut up! (The full stop prevents you drivelling on and undoing your case or diluting the effect. It also allows the other person space to take on board the implications of what you've just said.)

Rise to the occasion

If the other person is standing and you're sitting, stand up slowly and respectfully, eye to eye (that is, I to I).

Speak up

If they've been loud and you've been quiet, speak just a little more loudly than before, and see how this gets you noticed.

Be precise

It can be useful to ask the other person, coldly or neutrally, what exactly they are angry about and what exactly they need from you. Maybe you could do this at the time that they're 'doing' angry, or maybe sometime later – especially if they've already stomped off! – in a note or phone call.

Anxious people

who may also be Catastrophizers, Dejected, Miserable, Pessimists, Sad, Scared, Terrified, Timid, Unhappy or Worriers

What ticks us off

Some people just seem to be born worriers. They are always concerned about what *might* go wrong, and they can sometimes seem to obsess about it, rather than be able to get over it quickly. It's not exactly uplifting to be around someone who's doing this. And, for them, it's often very, very debilitating.

How it can happen

People often 'worry' because when a situation comes to mind, they have a single big picture in their mind of what has gone wrong in the past or what might go wrong in the future. This 'in-your-face' mental picture is too real, too compelling and too big for them to see beyond, or to be able to consider alternatives.

Sometimes it's because they hear or think something, rather than see something (eg a voice saying, 'this'll never work because...'), and this can also seem so definitive that it's hard to imagine otherwise.

(At times, the person might have several pictures or thoughts in mind, but these are often different facets of the same worst-case scenario.)

Tips for handling anxious people

The key is to help the person to see their picture, or hear their thought, as just one possibility rather than as an inevitability. For example, you might ask:

- 'What exactly are you concerned about?' to acknowledge their state of mind, and body. Allow plenty of time for them to feel comfortable to answer.
- 'What needs to happen to stop that (worse-case scenario) happening?'
- 'What are *all* the possible hurdles/barriers/problems you can foresee?' (And keep asking this until they run dry. This may generate alternative pictures or thoughts, to dilute the effect of their 'worrying' one, and begin to open their mind to other possibilities – albeit 'negative' ones for the time being. But they are all useful possibilities for you to consider, in any case.)
- 'In your opinion, what exactly needs to happen to help this to work, then?'
- 'How *probable* do you consider each of these possibilities to be – given our current situation, not past situations?' (This can help them to step back and assess the likelihood of the event happening, rather than simply to be over-whelmed by the very thought of it.)
- 'So, what exactly could go *right*?' (Be prepared to allow them time to think about this, or to get back to you, as this might not be their normal 'positive' pattern of thought.)

Apologetic people

who may feel so apologetic so often about so many things that they and others feel they're a 'Sorry' Person

What ticks us off

The best apology I ever heard was from a boss of mine. Someone had made a mistake that had cost our client dearly. He looked the client in the eye and said 'I've got three things to say to you.' (Pause)

The client stopped looking mightily embarrassed and turned to meet his gaze. 'Firstly, I'm sorry.' (Pause) 'We didn't mess this up deliberately.' (Pause) 'It was our mistake.' (Pause) 'Secondly, we will pay for any out-of-pocket expenses that this has cost your organization.' (Pause) 'We don't expect you to pay for our mistakes.' (Pause) 'And thirdly, I'm sure this has been a huge embarrassment for you personally.' (Short pause) 'Who do I need to speak to, to tell them that this was 100 per cent our fault? Sure, it was your responsibility to get us to do what your organization needs, but in this case you had done absolutely everything correctly, and I need your boss, or your boss's boss, to know that.' (Pause) The client let out the breath she had been holding all through this, and gratefully said just 'Thank you.'

Some people do the opposite of this. They don't just apologize, put the issue to bed and move on; they go on and on, and make matters worse.

How it can happen

When someone doesn't just apologize, but goes on and on, and makes matters worse, not only do other people have to cope with whatever is the subject of the apology, but they also can feel that they should be looking after the apologizer, who is getting themselves into a Sorry State! And they can see themselves having to help the apologizer to put themselves back together emotionally. Let's examine the strategies that people use to apologize *ineffectively*, which combine together to form the Sorry Cycle:

1. They don't talk simply about the event they are apologizing for, but avoid the issue with *external* excuses (eg 'I'd been made to work late and was tired'; 'the post was late'; 'other people made mistakes'), while often *internally* they are taking it very personally (eg 'I am stupid'; 'I shouldn't have done that'; 'I really should have foreseen that this might have gone wrong') or they are literally believing – in extreme cases – that they are a 'sorry' person. And as they are reminding themselves of all of this internally, at the same time as apologizing externally, they are making themselves feel worse, and embarrassing everyone else, which of course makes them feel worse.
2. They focus on what went wrong, rather than on what needs to happen now, which of course makes them feel worse still.
3. And they can end up not knowing what to say next, and so fill the embarrassed silence with tears or a rapid exit, which makes them feel even worse still.

Tips for handling apologetic people
Get them off the Sorry Cycle
If someone is over-apologizing to you, get them off the Sorry

Cycle by interrupting it. After they've said they're sorry, change the subject, eg 'Let me stop you there – I accept your apology, thanks. Now let's talk about damage limitation/next steps/the next item on the agenda.'

Be honest
A good tip for dealing with an overly apologetic person is to make succinct statements that cover:

- the situation;
- the other person's situation;
- your own situation.

Then change the subject.

For example, I remember a colleague saying to a co-worker, 'I'm sorry you're upset by this. That was not my intention. But my decision is still the same. For the good of the whole company. Any questions before we move on?' and the co-worker just said simply 'Er, no. Thank you.' (Each short point had been made. Each was accepted in turn. The matter was put to bed.)

Always change the subject immediately afterwards
If you leave a silence, then the other person may feel obliged to fill it. And they may be too emotional, lost in thought, or surprised that the apology is done and dusted so soon. Try, for example, 'So what do we need to do now?' or 'Thank you. Now the next item on the agenda, please?' or 'Let's meet for a drink later?'

When receiving an apology
- Look the person in the eye. (Otherwise, how can they *deliver* it effectively if no one is there to *receive* it?)
- Focus on future action, eg 'What needs to happen next?' 'What have you learnt that will be useful in future?' (After all, you are dealing with this at a *behavioural* level, not at a personal level, aren't you?)

■ Look the person in the eye again – check that they are OK, and address any needs they have (eg to take a short break to regain their composure or dignity after not receiving the expected humiliating dressing-down that would have achieved nothing anyway!).

Biased people

who may also be seen as Bigots, Closed-minded,
Prejudiced, Rigid, Unfair or Making Sweeping
Assumptions or Generalizations

What ticks us off

Sometimes people make sweeping assumptions based on generalizations:

- 'All foreigners are stupid.'
- 'She's always ill.'
- 'He'll never agree to this.'

And it's very hard to budge people with these biased attitudes.
(Whoops, another sweeping generalization! See how easy they
are to make and to have?)

How it can happen
Convincer strategy

Often, the person has a 'convincer strategy' of One. That is to
say, they only need an event to happen One time before they
feel convinced. This means that they love or hate something (a
proposal? a restaurant? a person?) on the basis of only one
example. For example, I myself have a convincer strategy of

One, so if someone has a cold the first time I meet them, I'm constantly thereafter tempted to enquire solicitously about their health!

'No foreign food'

Many years ago I took an elderly friend to see his wife in hospital. Afterwards I asked if he'd like to go and get something to eat. 'Yes please, anything will do', he said. As we passed various places I asked him, 'Indian?', then 'Chinese?', then 'Italian?', then 'French?' and so on, until he helped me a little by explaining that he didn't like 'foreign' food.

As we, eventually, were eating scrambled eggs on toast, he explained to me why he didn't like 'foreign food'. He had tried it once (he said) when he was involved in the evacuation of British soldiers from Dunkirk, and hadn't liked it at all, so had never eaten it in the 40 or so years since then.

Here's a clear 'convincer strategy' of One, where on one traumatic occasion during the Second World War, a lifetime's pattern was established.

I'm staying where I am

Some people's biases and prejudices come from taking only one perspective on a situation: their own. This can lead to what might seem very unfair decisions, because there are two other perspectives that they typically ignore: the other person's perspective, and an objective view of the overall situation.

They will tend to impose their map of the world on other people, albeit with the other person's interests at heart on occasions. For example, if their own hands are cold, they may well ask 'Aren't your hands cold?' or 'Don't you have any gloves?'

✓ **TIP**

Tips for handling biased people

If someone makes a sweeping generalization such as 'foreigners are stupid', they are almost certainly convinced that it's true. They might – if they are challenged – reply with something like 'Well, I met a foreigner once who couldn't understand a word of English' (which is a generalization born both from 1) a convincer strategy of One; *and* 2) from only their own perspective: ie if someone didn't understand me, they are obviously stupid!).

So, you could:

■ invite them to think a little below the surface by asking, very gently, 'Because...?';
■ challenge the generalization, gently, reflecting their words back as a gentle question, eg '*All* foreigners are stupid?' or 'She's *always* ill?' or 'He'll *never* agree to this?'

They might then reply with something like:

■ 'Well, I met a foreigner once who couldn't understand a word of English.'
■ 'Well, she's been off sick a couple of times recently.'
■ 'Well, he might agree, but I've never been able to persuade him yet.'

Then you could ask about the number of events this is based upon:

■ 'How many foreigners are you basing this on?'
■ 'How many times has she been ill, and over what period of time?'
■ 'How many times has he disagreed with something like this, out of a total of how many?'

Broaden the context (ie widen out the experience base they are drawing upon), eg:

■ 'Do you think that "foreign" doctors, scientists, teachers and nurses are more stupid than others?'
■ 'What examples can you think of, of when she was in good health?'
■ 'Have you never seen him agree with anything?'

The 'magic question'

I'm very fond of the 'magic question', as it opens up the situation hypothetically, not challengingly: 'What would have to happen for you to reconsider this opinion?' (Or you might feel brave enough to personalize it, and ask about 'your' opinion instead of 'this' opinion.)

A useful follow-up to whatever they reply – and you might want to give them time to consider it – could then be 'And would you be willing to give that a try?' and/or 'What help/support/resources would you need to do that?'

Changing places

If a decision/generalization/assumption is made unfairly, and you can see that the other person has made this only from their own perspective and has not taken all factors into account, you might get them to broaden their view not by challenging them aggressively, but by saying something like 'I can see, from your point of view, why Z seems fair, but – putting yourself in my shoes – could you also take X and Y into consideration, so that I can feel comfortable with it too?'

And then, after a pause while this sinks in, but before they have a chance to object, offer a solution that works for both of you, eg 'How about I do A, which will achieve the X and Y that I need, and the Z that you asked for as well?'

Blamers

who may Blame Other People or Blame
Circumstances, or just Not Take Responsibility for
their own actions

What ticks us off

'It wasn't me. It was them. Honest. They messed it up. I did warn them, but would they listen to me?' And on and on they go. This might sound familiar?

Another pattern is just a curt 'It wasn't me.' And both are normally accompanied by abnormal eye contact (eg over-intense, shifting or none at all), and an abnormal tone of voice (eg clipped, desperate or tight).

We can often sense a tightness and even panic in the person who is denying responsibility – whether they are going on at length about it or just flatly denying it. So, we have to deal with their panic and avoidance, as well as the situation!

How it can happen

Often this blaming happens because the person finds it hard to accept responsibility for what they've done or to apologize for the effects of what they've done. Maybe they take personally what they did wrong, as a reflection of who they *are* (eg instead of stopping at 'I got that wrong', they automatically add something like '... so it proves I am stupid, again'). Maybe they've suffered punishments in the past for making mistakes, and are avoiding the possibility of punishment again? Maybe they've been told that it's a sign of weakness to apologize or accept responsibility? Whatever the reasons or the causes, their blaming seems almost like an automatic reaction.

Tips for handling blamers

Culture shift

Whatever organization we're dealing with – a team, a business, a hospital, a school, a family – the key is to establish a safe culture of responsibility-without-blame. This is easy so long as we focus on future activities and leave people's identities (ie who they are) and feelings out of the equation. (This might puzzle or even shock people who've been used to blame and punishment, so be prepared if they need a bit of time for it to sink in.) We hear a lot about establishing a 'blame-free' culture, but how can it be done? Here are some tried and tested ways:

- Break the pattern of protestation by interrupting them if necessary. Stop them 'doing' blaming, however they do it.
- Focus on the future, and what needs to happen.
- Try 'Forget what has happened; what exactly needs to be achieved?'
- You may need to give them time to come back to you on this, but when you have the outcomes clearly agreed, you can then ask them, or agree with them, *how* exactly the outcomes could be achieved, and by whom, by when, and with what resources and support.
- Learn by reflecting: ensure that each person involved thinks about what they'll do differently as a result of what they've learnt from this episode. Some people will benefit from doing this one-to-one. Some teams or groups will benefit

from doing it together. Or a combination of the two might work. (Not only does this reflection enhance the overall learning of the individuals and the team, but also it demonstrates that punishment is not necessarily the best way to function.)

'Blaming everyone else'

We were running a big workshop called 'How to Handle Situations You Can't Handle' and at the start we asked the group what they wanted from the day. Various of the 100-plus group stood up and explained why they were there, and then one man shot up to his feet, banged the table and exploded 'I'm sick and tired of my situation! I hate my job. I hate the people I work with. I want to do something about it!' Stunned silence ensued.

Anyway, at the end of the day we asked if anyone had anything they wanted to say to the group, and our friend drifted to his feet, and dreamily explained 'I said this morning that I wanted to change my situation, but I haven't achieved that, and it doesn't really matter any more...' and you could have heard a pin drop as we waited expectantly for what he was going to say next. He continued, 'I've realized today that I can't change my situation, but that if I change *in* my situation, then (long pause) my situation has changed...!' – and he sat dreamily back onto his seat.

His enormous realization about taking responsibility caused a massive shift in his attitude. Gone was his hostility towards the world. And he had the tools to change – not his 'self', but his behaviours.

Boring people

who may also be Burblers, Digressers, Ramblers, Tedious, Unfocused or Wafflers

What ticks us off

Do they get straight to the point? Do they interest you with their conversation? Do you look forward to meeting with them? Do you heck – you get a sinking feeling even thinking about them! Off they go again, talking and talking but not really saying anything, while the rest of us are twiddling our thumbs, wondering when, or if, they are ever going to get to The Point, as they, sort of, if you know what I mean, go on and on – oh, and, by the way, popping off on little detours from time to time, and then, very often, stopping and asking something like 'Sorry, what was I saying?'!

This all wastes time, energy and attention. It labels people as 'boring' whose expertise might be undervalued. (In one company I worked with, a colleague was labelled 'the company anaesthetist'. When I asked why, I was told that whenever they opened their mouth, other people fell asleep!)

How it can happen

There are several possible strategies they use:

■ Some people just need to *think aloud*, and until they hear what they have to say, they don't really know what they think. (This can be wearing for the rest of us!)

■ Others simply have not clarified 'inside' what they want to communicate 'outside'. (Hence the old wives' tale 'Engage brain before opening mouth.') They don't really know what they are trying to say – through a lack of pre-planning – and so they do the thinking whilst in the meeting. It's pressured for them, and pointless for the rest of the people.

■ Others are 'detail' people rather than 'big picture' people, and they keep on giving details until they run out.

■ And others may consider themselves to be 'creative', giving endless possibilities at every opportunity.

■ Eye contact is often with the ceiling or floor, rather than with the people in the room, as they are thinking aloud and unready to talk to people. (This makes it somewhat impossible for them to see that they are boring people, and to change their course of action.) Sometimes, however, their eye contact is intense, as they realize they are talking aloud and try to over-compensate. At other times, if they realize that they are boring others, they intensify whatever they are doing and make matters worse, for example by speeding up (making what they say boring *and unintelligible*) or by getting louder (making it boring *and embarrassing*) or by over-justifying their case (making it boring *and repetitive*) or by giving too much detail (making it boring *and confusing*).

 ✓ TIP

Tips for handling boring people

What all of these varieties of boring people have in common is that those responsible are not noticing the effect they are having on others until it's too late. And frequently at the same time, they are saying to themselves something like 'What on earth am I talking about?! Where on earth am I going with this?! Will someone help me, PLEASE!'

Bored, bored, bored

If you are being bored, say so, nicely. Take ownership of feeling bored, rather than blaming the other person. For example: 'I need to stop you as I'm feeling confused with too much detail.' Or 'Can I remind you that we agreed to your proposal a few minutes ago? You can stop now.' Or 'I need to take a break – I'm feeling overloaded and can't concentrate.'

The first step is to look them in the eye and stop them (ie rescue them) firmly but gently. Using their name followed by a pause is often effective and simple, eg 'Mike.' (Pause to get Mike's attention...)

The next step is to rescue them kindly by 1) recognizing the situation; and 2) pointing the way forward. For example: 'Mike.' (Pause) 'I'm not clear where you're going with this yet.' (Pause, while Mike gratefully stops!) 'Could we give you a few minutes to think further on the precise points you want to make, and come back to you?' (Note the clear offer/instruction to come up with 'precise points' to help Mike to focus.)

You might also give them a more precise brief, eg 'We only need a headline recommendation from you, in no more than 30 seconds', or 'Let's leave the details until later and just hear your key points, please' or, simply and honestly, 'I'm not sure we've time to do this justice. How about you e-mail us the bullet points after the meeting, for us to consider next time?'

Be clear and say what you want them to do next, eg 'Please can you just give us your recommendation? We'll take on trust your thinking, and we'll ask any questions if we have them' or 'I need to know in a nutshell...' or 'After a break, let's come back to this and spend just five minutes more.'

But the best strategy is to avoid being bored in the first place. Nowadays I always specify in advance – to financial advisers, presenters, salespeople, etc – what I *need*. For example: 'Can you please give me the big picture/bottom line first, in only one sentence, and then I can ask you any questions this raises for me?' or 'My brain can't take in details unless it knows what to do with them. So can you please start with your final conclusions and recommendations?'

Agendas

I tend to ask people to tell me in advance of a meeting how long they need for each item on the agenda, to find out what time each item needs to start and finish, and therefore to find out how long the meeting 'needs' to be.

This enables us to negotiate in advance the level of detail that 1) they need to give; and 2) we need to suffer – sorry, hear. In this way, expectations are clearly agreed in advance, and any items that might take an excessive time can be avoided – eg by asking for a briefing paper in advance. And, again, I will always negotiate the level of detail that is needed in a paper, to avoid the same situation occurring in writing.

And, importantly for me, I will avoid those parts of the meeting where I don't need to be there, and ask for those parts I want to be at to be clustered together so I:

■ don't need to keep popping in and out;
■ don't get bored by being there when I don't need to be there.

'Me too'

A story I heard from a counsellor/therapist – which drew gasps of astonishment from his audience initially – illustrates the benefits of getting the boredom out in the open, so it can be dealt with. He was working with a client and just couldn't keep his eyes open. Eventually, after fidgeting, walking back and forth, sipping his water, going for a 'comfort break' – none of which had resuscitated his interest – he said to his client 'I feel so bored and unable to concentrate: is it just me, or are you feeling it too?'

The client looked both astonished and relieved. 'Yes, yes, I do, and thank you so much for mentioning it because I've noticed that I have this effect on people but because no one's ever felt able to mention it to me, I've never felt comfortable to mention it myself and...' Our counsellor/therapist friend interrupted him and suggested that they both take a break and then *come* back to consider what to do next.

Stating the obvious often hits the nail, very precisely, on the head!

7

Bullies

*who may also be Aggressive, Belittling, Bombastic,
Bossy, Dictatorial, Haranguing, Harassing,
Intimidating, Oppressive, Pressurizing, Railroading,
Threatening or plain Unkind or quite possibly all
of these at once*

What ticks us off

In a nutshell, what annoys us, to put it mildly, is feeling bullied.
And however 'grown up' we may be, we can feel belittled,
marginalized, ignored, insignificant – the list goes on and on –
at quite a profound personal level.

And the hurt goes on and on, too. I bet we can all remember
the person who bullied us, whether physically or mentally,
recently or long, long ago, and still feel resentful, and
revengeful.

How it can happen

We're not talking here about the teasing between friends that is
pleasurable, inoffensive and acceptable to both parties. We're
talking behaviour that crosses the line and is, for at least
one party, unpleasant, offensive and unacceptable. This can be
verbal, physical and/or emotional bullying.

The major motivation for most bullies is that they can only
feel 'big' (or 'significant' or 'alive' or 'real') when they make

others feel 'small'. And – though this is no excuse – the bully is very often being bullied themselves, or has been, so this is the only way they know to gain some self-esteem for themself.

How do they do this? There are many ways:

- Being physically violent.
- Threatening to be physically violent.
- Playing 'mind-games' that make the victim feel 'small', eg threatening to make the victim suffer status-wise – for example: 'You wouldn't want (the boss) to think that you weren't up to the job, would you?'
- Making things personal – for example, instead of saying something like 'You didn't present that very confidently, did you? How might you do it differently next time?' they might say 'Yet again you've proved to everyone that you're a really pathetic presenter.'

Tips for handling bullies

You must (and this is one of only a handful of times I use the word 'must') talk with *at least* one other person about what's been happening to you. It doesn't matter who it is, so long as you can trust them, and it may be better if they have nothing to do with the specific situation. You need at least one person who is not connected with the situation but who is there for *you*. After all, the only thing worse than feeling bullied is to feel bullied and alone.

What you think of me is not who I am

As a vital form of self-protection, remember that whoever or whatever they say you 'are' or 'aren't' (however violently they may say it), this is:

- only their opinion;
- based on what you did or said;

- not on who you are as a person;
- and you can easily change what you say or do, *if* you want to.

'Cathy's screen'

I knew someone who, whenever she was feeling bullied, had her thick glass screen rise out of the floor between her and the bully. She explained that she could see and hear them perfectly, but that all of their 'stuff' just stayed on their side of the screen and didn't 'get to her'. That way, she could listen and respond calmly, without feeling whatever they were trying to get her to feel.

Having taught this idea to many people, I've been impressed by the varieties of screen that people have adopted:

- one that curves up over the head, because we get a lot of 'stuff' dumped on us from above;
- a 360-degree screen, because 'people tend to try stabbing you in the back around here';
- a Berlin Wall-like thick one, 'to keep me feeling safe no matter what's thrown at me';
- one with built-in volume and size and colour controls so 'I can turn down whatever's overpowering, and feel comfortable and in control'.

Whatever works, works! This is an easy, cheap and fun form of self-protection.

Focus on the future

Ask something practical (not personal) like 'So how exactly do you think I might do it differently next time?' and notice that this:

- asks for their opinion, thus showing them that you've heard them;
- stays firmly on what you might do or say, rather than anything 'personal';

■ gets them to look constructively to the future, not destructively to the past;
■ gives you some genuinely useful pointers – not to follow slavishly, but to consider.

Then – and this might seem a bit odd – thank them for their suggestions and tell them that you'll consider them (because there might well be some useful ideas in there).

This keeps them talking, but on your terms, not theirs. It shows that you're not scared of them and are willing to talk as an equal (and it may have been a long, long time since someone's done that with them, or shown them how to do it).

Continue a dialogue with them

Over time, give them some feedback on their suggestions and add in some of your own. This will show your respect for their suggestions (if not for their previous behaviours!) and give every bully what they crave: being noticed and acknowledged and, in these scenarios, feeling genuinely useful.

Not here, you don't!

Another approach is to follow, clearly, a legal or disciplinary route with the aid of your line manager and/or union or professional body. (You may also involve your line manager's line manager if your line manager has been causing the problem.) Most countries now have anti-bullying procedures and/or legislation for the protection of people in the workplace. We can all expect to be allowed to do our job without fear of being bullied, threatened or harassed.

Unfortunately, however, someone who follows these paths might be branded a 'whistleblower' or 'sneak' or simply unable to look after themselves, and so these more formal routes should be considered very carefully before being followed.

There is, however, strength in numbers, and if your union or professional body representative – or even your co-workers – are willing to work with you, a joint approach to the bully can work wonders. *Not* to threaten the bully, because that can easily escalate out of control, but to discuss – at a calm moment – how their behaviour has been causing upset, and how exactly they might behave differently. They might even be offered some form of coaching to help them.

What/how

A specific way of feeling subtly bullied or railroaded into doing something is for the person who is briefing you to tell you not only *what* to do, but *how* you 'should' do it – for example: 'By Friday lunchtime I need a report on X, so you'll need to ring these people, visit those people and do a spreadsheet in order to get the results.'

Well, there might be other ways of doing it that are easier or quicker for you. But it's easy to feel railroaded into 'having' to do it the way that you've been told to, instead of finding your own way of doing it. (This may not be the most overt form of bullying, but it can leave someone feeling very belittled when they have to keep going back to ask for guidance on how exactly they are supposed to carry out the task.)

'What? How?'

I remember a young colleague coming trembling out of his boss's office. 'He's told me to do X, Y and Z by Tuesday at 3 pm and I don't know how to!'

I pointed out that – from what I'd heard – he'd only been told to do X, but the Y and Z were *how* the boss would have done it himself. I suggested that the young trembler think about *how* he himself could achieve X, and then check back with his boss.

He thought about it, went to see the boss and said 'I just want to check with you before I start that what you want is X by Tuesday at 3 pm? You suggested I do it by doing Y and Z, which I don't know how to do. Is it OK to do A and B instead, which will give you the same result?' And after a short pause for thought, the boss simply said 'Of course.'

Unless there is a specific procedure that *has* to be followed – for safety purposes, say – most people don't care *how* something is done.

Sticks and stones

It is said that 'Sticks and stones can break my bones, but words can never hurt me.' All I can say to this is 'Rubbish!' Verbal bullying, belittling, appearance bullying – whatever it's called – can be taken very personally and very painfully.

To respond in a positive way, remember that the insult might have been meant personally, but you can choose not to take it that way. For example, a response that 'fogs' the bully's intention might be 'And your point is…?' or 'And so you're asking me… what, exactly?'

8

Change-resistant people

who may also be Conservative, Inflexible, Risk-averse, Unadventurous, Unimaginative or indeed just Calm and Patient

What ticks us off

Some people look terrified even at the inkling that change may be about to happen. Indeed, even just the word 'change' can cause real panic in people. They can close right down, worrying about the very worst that might happen.

And as change continues to happen more and more, resistance to change needs to be managed.

How it can happen

Those people who think negatively of change are unlikely to think of pay rises, birthday presents or other positive changes. The word 'change' seems for them to carry connotations of '... for the worse'. And so they can close down and refuse even to consider the possibilities, because they are too preoccupied 'doing' terrified, inside, and mentally reliving whatever disasters have happened in the past, and – they imagine – might well happen again.

'Off the beaten path'

I was chatting to a taxi driver about a recent bus strike in London, and asked how it had affected his business. I had expected him to be pleased about the increase in numbers of people using his taxi instead of a bus, but no!

'I hate bus strikes', he said. 'I get no end of complaints from people when I take them on the shortest route to avoid all the extra traffic caused by people using their cars instead of buses. They get really anxious and want me to stay exactly on the roads that their bus normally takes!'

Certainly, a small level of anxiety about change or taking risks or the unknown is very normal, as it raises our level of adrenaline to be able cope with it. This 'anxiety' is, I repeat, very normal. But for some people it has become a genuine phobia where, at the mere thought of change, they have horribly vivid images of what could go wrong or what has gone wrong in the past. The idea manages them, and they are unable to manage 'it'.

And indeed for many people, the longer they are even mildly anxious about the unknown, the more likely they are to develop a phobia. After all, they will have a longer time to imagine what might happen (ie turn out 'for the worst' for them).

 TIP

Tips for handling change-resistant people

Change-resistant, risk-averse people are not being bloody-minded just to obstruct progress. Well, actually they are! They are literally reminding themselves of past events where they have been bloodied – metaphorically, at least.

Change is...

As a revealing exercise, you might like to try this on other people, or even on yourself – just complete these four sentences instinctively with the first things that pop into your head:

- Change is...
- Change isn't...
- If only Change were more...
- If only Change were less...

People who fear change might come up with something that reflects really deep fears, like:

- Change is scary...
- Change isn't safe...
- If only Change were more infrequent...
- If only Change were less unsettling...

Respect

Start by respecting their anxiety or phobia – for example: 'I understand you may have had some horrible experiences of bad changes in the past, sometimes dressed up in the guise of "opportunities" or "improvements", but I'd like you to put those past events to one side and consider all the possibilities – negative and positive – about how it might be if we were to...?'

Ask for problems

Maybe you could dive straight into the deep end, beyond their generalized 'Change is scary' into 'So what, *exactly*, would be scary about that – point by point, please? We need to think about and address all aspects, don't we?'

And then you might ask 'And what could we do to make the situation *less* scary?' Perhaps you could do this with small groups of people, to stimulate ideas and depersonalize it somewhat for the individuals, compared to a one-on-one environment.

Check the baby

Sometimes, just sometimes, they might be right! Change, with the best intentions in the world, might just be for the sake of it, and it's too easy to throw out the baby with the bathwater. (A very successful Canadian beer once advertised with the slogan 'Tired of the same old beer? Nope. Nor are we.')

9

Charmers

*who may also be Attractive, Charismatic,
Seductive, Slick, Slimy or Smarmy or quite possibly
all of these together*

What ticks us off

There's nothing wrong with genuine charm (ie *how* something is done, with politeness, warmth, consideration for others), but some people habitually and hollowly charm their way into and out of any situation. They leave others to pick up the pieces and may feign surprise at the mess or hurt they have left behind, or may even be genuinely surprised, so automatic is their behaviour.

How it can happen

Charm and charisma often develop in people whom other people find 'attractive'. And the people who are attracted to them, for whatever reason, are therefore motivated to want to 'get to know' them. So, have you ever noticed how 'attractive' people rarely start a true conversation, or need to? That's because they are used to people who find them attractive initiating the conversations. And, in turn, that's largely why 'attractive' people can become accustomed to being able to say and do almost anything, and get away with it! (The more astute ones are well aware of the power this brings, and are conscious of the potential to misuse this power. The others just enjoy the attention and even adulation that they receive, irrespective of the consequences, which they are barely aware of in any case – because they're being admired by their *next* admirer!)

Back to charmers – do they never initiate true conversations, you might be asking? Well, not really. They might have conversation *starters*, such as 'Tell me about yourself' or 'What can we do for you?', but these are designed to draw out the other person's agenda, which they can then fit in with. And that's why they can develop a habit of saying whatever they think the other person might find the most charming.

They might then promise them the earth, to keep the attraction going, even if it's not theirs to give. Or – in organizations – they might over-promise what the organization cannot deliver.

Challenge them on this – for example: 'Mike, how on earth could you promise that we would do X?' and you might get an innocent 'But I thought that's what they wanted.' And you know the irritating thing – they are probably right! Years of charming has left them with good instincts for what other people would like, or at least would like to hear.

Many CEOs, politicians and entrepreneurs are utterly brilliant at being charming. In fact, that's their main skill, and there's nothing wrong with that so long as they have a team to deal with the detail. Think of Prince Charming. Charming is all he was required to do, and by all accounts he did it brilliantly. (What is less well known is that in the palace there were others to take care of the business.)

Tips for handling charmers

Cinderella's fella

Consider again Prince Charming; he is a good example of a

charmer, and was most definitely not brought up as Prince Team Player. *Being* charming has become an embedded part of who charmers consider they, deep down, are. So, the following are very unlikely to work:

- getting them to be a team player;
- asking them to consider consequences in advance;
- requesting that they consult before committing;
- suggesting that they themselves deliver what they have promised.

Play to the charmer's strength – finding out what other people really want by charming it out of them. Wind them up and point them in the direction of the new, or the unfathomable. Get them to soothe someone who's upset or disillusioned or disenchanted. What you might find hard, but with practice it will happen (possibly over a jolly drink rather than by asking directly), is to get them to tell you what they've discovered! (They are used to other people making the running, not stopping to analyse and explain what's going on.)

So, accept the fact that they may leave people charmed, and that you might have to go along and apologize for their over-promise, but they will have bought you all a lot of goodwill in the meantime. (And yes, you're right – some people will see through this in a trice, and may well give you marks for trying, but will not fall for the charm or be won over. But since this situation was unfathomable to begin with, you've lost nothing in any case, have you?)

10

Cold people

*who may also be seen as Thick-skinned,
Unaffectionate, Unemotional, Unempathetic,
Uninvolved or possibly even Insensitive or Brutal*

What ticks us off

People who radiate coldness are often referred to as 'fridges'. That's how they 'are'.

They typically don't want to get involved, or even can't risk or face getting involved, with other people. To be honest, they are the last people we would go to if we had a personal problem; they'd maybe just stare at us in blank amazement, or scuttle off to some hurriedly remembered appointment. In any case, they probably choose careers where dealing with people is low on the agenda – and might well feel more comfortable dealing with numbers or machines.

We don't particularly, therefore, welcome them into our teams, or hearts. They may be described functionally as useful or hard-working, but they are rarely thought of or talked about emotionally or affectionately.

How it can happen

There are many reasons *why* this may happen: having been hurt in the past, not wanting to blur the boundaries between work and outside, fear of over-involvement, being wary of identifying with the problem. But *how* it happens is much simpler.

Second person

Empathy, warmth and affection emerge when people are good at putting themselves in others' shoes and imagining what things are like for the other (ie second) person. They might say things like 'From the way you describe it, that must have hurt you' or 'By the smile on your face, you are obviously feeling very proud.' (Some people can overdo this, however, and *crowd* into the other person's shoes, saying things like 'I know *just* how you feel.')

These people *don't* normally 'do' cold, unless they are flung out of the other person's shoes, perhaps for having been too emotionally crowding, and then they might withdraw as a reaction.

First person

Some people are very aware of themselves (ie first person) and what's going on in their own shoes, eg 'I'm angry', 'I'm confused', 'I need to speak my mind'. They are rarely seen as cold, even though people might be a little wary of getting involved with them. Sure, they know what they like, and where they stand, but that might leave little room for other people to relate to them.

Third person

Some people just want the facts in a situation – for example: 'Forget about what I feel, just show me the facts, please' or 'I'm not interested that you believe in this – where is the evidence?'

This 'third person' position can be interpreted as 'coldness', because the response comes from no one's shoes; it comes from a detached observer position, looking objectively at the shoe shop, so to speak.

Sometimes the person might deliberately load on the coldness as a barrier, but a matter-of-fact tone of voice can easily be interpreted as cold or clinical in itself.

Tips for handling cold people

Forcing a 'cold' person to get more involved, or to give a personal opinion, might well be frustrating (for both of you) and fruitless. (The saying that comes to mind is 'Never try to teach a pig to fly – you won't succeed, it'll be really hard work, and you'll really annoy the pig'.) They might in any case find it hard to know what they do 'feel' in their own shoes, preferring to think 'about' the situation, rather than go 'into' it. This is not to say that they don't have feelings – but they might well have chosen not to allow themselves to 'feel'. And this choice demands a lot of energy and willpower (won't-power?) to maintain their position, façade or front – whatever they have chosen. And maintain it they will, at all costs, because if it were to crumble and they were to 'go to pieces' because of unmanageable feelings, they often fear that it might not be possible to pick up all the pieces. (Of course, they *might* surprise you with huge resources of empathy and warmth on a personal matter, but if that happens and these floodgates of theirs are unleashed, be prepared to help with their embarrassment and confusion at this unleashing and loss of 'face'.)

When in Rome...

So, in a nutshell, speak *their* language. They've clearly shown *how* they prefer to communicate, so do what they do.

If you want their opinion, ask for their 'analysis'. If you want to know how they feel about something, ask about the 'pros and cons'. If you want to get them involved, ask them to be available as and when their input may be needed. You get the picture?

11

Competitive people

What ticks us off

Competitive people always have to be the winner, at the front of the line, or have the last word, the best results, the biggest desk – or at least they need to be *seen* to be the winner. This can be pretty tiring for other people if they try to keep up with them – and it's pretty exhausting for them too, as they put their everything into winning.

How it can happen

These people are not just show-offs who crave attention, since they genuinely love the chase, race, battle and challenge. In fact, they *need* it and *thrive* on it. (*This* reminds me of a car bumper sticker I once saw saying 'Whoever Dies with the Most Designer Clothes *Wins*.' Some people seem absolutely compelled or driven to win at *everything*.)

Tips for handling competitive people

There may be many reasons why they feel and behave like this, but whatever the reasons, these people are reasonably easy to handle.

Here's a challenge for you!

If these people need the thrill of the chase, it's easy to give it to them, or to give them that impression. They'll love even relatively everyday tasks packed in a shiny wrapping – for example:

- ■ 'I'm not sure if you'll be able to crack this one, but...'
- ■ 'Do you think that X would be better at doing this than you, or will you accept the challenge?'
- ■ 'I've no idea whether this is possible, but...'
- ■ 'I'm not sure if this can be done in time, but would you have a go?'
- ■ 'I've no one else to turn to/rely on for this.'

And the winner is... (Part 1)

Praise them. Be precise about what they've achieved against all the odds. If they prefer to be praised publicly, ensure that you do it in the way that best pleases them. If they prefer to be praised privately (as many people do), I'd be very, very surprised!

And the winner is... (Part 2)

Praise everyone. It's only fair, and who *doesn't* like it? And ensure that you make a modest mention of those you praise in private to Our Competitive Friends, so that they don't get to feel complacent and are energized by the sense of competition.

League tables

It's perfectly possible to have Our Competitive Friends motivated by all sorts of performance charts on a weekly or monthly, or even daily or hourly, basis, so long as other people don't feel left out or left behind.

You might confide the results only to those who are energized by them, and not bother those who aren't bothered.

You might also confide to those who aren't bothered, why exactly you're doing this, as you hope to motivate each person in the way they prefer to be motivated, rather than in a uniform way.

12

Confused people

who may also be Unsettled

What ticks us off

If someone is confused, their feelings of being unsettled can unsettle others. They look unsettled. They can't concentrate. And they often feel they shouldn't be confused, which only adds to their confusion.

How it can happen

It can feel very unsettling for someone to 'be' confused. Inside, their head may be swirling. Their ears and eyes may be open but they may not really hear or see. They may feel less solid and secure than usual. Or their chest may feel tight and panicky as they desperately need to be able to breathe freely again. In extreme cases they might even 'go to pieces'.

Some people even feel that 'being confused' is like 'being stupid', whereas in fact confusion is an essential step in most learning processes. (It could also be thought of as 'playing with ideas' when we're deliberately playing with thought fragments.)

All this is very natural. Confusion is like having jigsaw puzzle pieces without the big picture, or like having the ingredients without a recipe – it's not clear what we are supposed to do with them. Or worse still, when we have a lot 'on our mind' it can be like having the ingredients to several recipes, without the recipes! Without a pattern, we can play with the pieces this way and that, time and time again, with little hope of resolution.

Confusion is sometimes not having all the pieces. Sometimes it's being unsure whether or not there are pieces missing. And at other times it's sensing that the pieces you were sure of have been disturbed or rearranged. In all cases we can get uptight because we are confused, or we can let the pieces just 'be' there, until resolution happens.

New or changed information

Sometimes we 'become' confused when someone says or does something that seems out of character or unexpected (ie from a different 'pattern'). How can we accommodate this new information in a pattern that now suddenly seems outdated?

An extreme example might be when someone does something negative and surprises us with the information that even though they pretended to be our friend, they never really liked us. It's left to us to re-examine history and to make sense of the events from the 'friend' pattern, in the context of this new 'pretending to be a friend' pattern.

Collecting information

At the beginning of a project we may have a sense of *what* we want to achieve, but have no idea of *how* we might achieve it. So, we are playing with lots of potential patterns, one after another, or at the same time. Again these can get confused, with each other.

Conflicting information

Often we might have two pieces of information that do not easily coexist in the same pattern, eg 'I need you (a work colleague) to draft a Dear John letter to my girlfriend/boyfriend for me' (ie a Personal Pattern within a Work Pattern).

Tips for handling confused people

As complex and confusing as confusion itself feels, it's simple to exit from it. Here are some tried and tested questions.

What exactly are you confused about?

This question generally helps to pin down the issue because, to answer it, the person has to search through all the pieces they are playing with, to identify, by elimination, the precise problem areas.

What exactly do you need?

This is a simple question that will often receive something like 'I don't know' as an initial answer. Give the person time to think about this, because if the answer had been an easy one, they would have sorted out the situation for themselves.

Other variations on this are 'What exactly are you missing?' or 'What exactly would solve this for you?' (But you'd probably not be helping by asking 'What can I do?', because the issue is 'what needs to be done', rather than who could do it. That can come later.)

'Clearly getting less confused'

The story comes to mind of someone who was asked a question and then started thinking aloud, at length. The questioner got impatient with the lack of an immediate precise answer, and said so. The 'thinker aloud' replied 'I'm still confused, so how do I know what I think, until I hear what I have to say?'!

A lot of people are like this. They produce ideas through their mouth in order to edit them through their ears. This is quite an efficient process, so long as they warn people, eg by saying 'Let me think...' or 'I just need to think aloud on this...' or 'I'm going to think aloud, so you can carry on with what you're doing as I don't need you to participate in this!'

13

Difficult people

who may be plain Contrary, Disagreeable or
Disharmonious

What ticks us off

Some people 'are' just difficult, we hear. It's not just one aspect of their behaviour, it's 'them' as a person. If I said black was black, they'd say it was white. If I said this book was a book, they'd disagree. And it's common for this contrariness to be mutual – as the saying goes, 'When you think you're dealing with an idiot, so do they!'

How it can happen

Physiologically, when this pattern exists between two people, or between one person in a group and the rest of the group, our body language involuntarily shows us to be tensing up in preparation for whatever battle is to come, and so the other person sees us tensed up for battle. A self-fulfilling prophecy. (Try it on for size: think of someone you've had problems with and say to yourself 'This is going to be difficult, again.' You can feel your shoulders sagging, your energy dropping and your spirits drooping, can't you?)

Shared values, however, can lead to harmony (for example, we can still be very good friends even with someone whose behavioural likes and dislikes are very different from our own, as we can 'agree to differ').

Dissimilar values, though, can generally lead to severe disharmony because of battles of 'realities' (eg 'Well, I need X!', 'Well, I need Y!' or 'Well, I believe X!', 'Well, I believe Y!'). And fundamentally there is often an obstructive belief that is based on past experiences, much like 'This is going to be difficult, again' or 'This person is difficult' – which dooms past events to repeat themselves, especially if we've been thinking of them:

■ in the future or present tense rather than in the past tense, eg 'they are never interested in what I have to say' versus 'they *have never been* interested in what I've had to say'; and/or

■ as the whole person or situation being 'difficult' (rather than one aspect of their behaviour *having been* difficult as against 'them' being difficult as a person), and this perpetuates the situation, eg 'they are difficult' or 'they'll never be able to do this'.

Tips for handling difficult people

Stay neutral

Rather than dismiss the whole person or situation as inevitably continuing to be 'difficult', contain the behaviour (not the person) in the past tense, not the future or present tense, in order to leave room for a different course of action. For example, instead of saying to yourself 'They'll never be able to do this', try something like 'They've never been able to do this...' and maybe add '... so I'd better find out what's been stopping them, and what needs to happen differently.'

Sharing clashing values

Clashing values can have profound effects. One person may 'need' something that's very contradictory to what another person needs. Nothing can ever shift either side, whatever is tried. (Notice the *awful* use of future and present tenses, dooming this situation to perpetual 'failure'!)

So let's rephrase it – 'Nothing has ever shifted either side, whatever has been tried' – thereby leaving the field wide open to try new things. And maybe try this simple three-step negotiation process:

1. What exactly do you need, in this situation? (And keep eliciting 'What else?')
2. What exactly do *I* need, in this situation? (Ditto.)
3. How exactly could we get what we both need, so that neither of us feels compromised, and we get a truly comprehensive solution?

14

Disobedient people

What ticks us off

How many times do I have to tell them! Why can't they listen?!
Why can't they do as they're told?! They tell you one thing and
then go off and do another! And so on – it can be exasperating
and exhausting and, above all, bewildering! Why can't people
just do as they're asked to do?! (And this applies just as much
to people who do more than they're asked to do, as well as less,
or nothing.)

How it can happen
No negatives please

The first pattern that ensures that things turn out exactly as we
don't want them to is to tell people what we *don't* want. Think
about it. How can you guarantee that children will run in
school corridors, or that a person will worry about something?
Easy. Tell them 'Don't run in the corridors' or 'Don't worry.'

Try it for yourself. Don't think of a pink elephant whistling.
Don't think of a lovely sandy beach under a deep blue sky.

The way that 'Don't...' works is to freeze the thought
processes, similarly to 'Stop...' or 'I don't want you to...' or one
of the many other forms of thought stoppers. And what does
the brain do once stopped? Nothing. It simply obeys the

instruction. It's the same as if you shout 'Don't!!!' at someone who's doing something; they freeze, wondering what they are supposed not to do or to stop doing.

What happens next is that the brain gratefully seizes on whatever it is given next, so that it can start doing something again, but doing what? That's easy: '... run in the corridors' or '... worry' or '... think of a pink elephant whistling' or '... think of a lovely sandy beach under a deep blue sky'.

I thought you said...

Another pattern is that some people take on too much responsibility because they regard information as instructions, whereas others take too little responsibility as they regard instructions purely as information.

Hearing information as instructions

These people are eager to please, and to go the extra mile – even if not asked or not required to do so. Have you ever asked someone something simple, such as 'Can you find out train times to Smalltown on Friday morning?' only to find that they later hand you a ticket?! And when you point out that you were just wondering about the journey times, they'll be adamant that you asked them to fix the journey for you? Or have you ever made a simple observation, eg 'This room looks a little grubby', only to find that they are convinced you told them to clean it or redecorate it?

Hearing instructions as information

The opposite pattern is where you think you have told someone explicitly what you need, and by when. You have checked that they understand how to go about it, but not only do they miss the deadline, they seem oblivious to whatever they had agreed to, eg 'I thought we were just chatting about it – you didn't tell me to do anything. Honestly, I'd have remembered!' And they truly believe this! It can seem as though they are just drifting around, never actually coming down to earth.

Tips for handling disobedient people

There are a few ways to ensure that we get what we want.

Don't don't(!)

Going completely against the way that the 'don't' pattern works, tell people clearly *what to do*, not what not to do. In this way you'll be planting the thought of what you want, rather than of what you don't want.

'Why do people fear dentists?'

I remember giving a workshop on this language pattern to a group of dentists. They use it a lot. Instead of saying things like 'This drilling will be quick' or 'This will be a little uncomfortable' or 'Think of nice things', they might be using language like 'This drilling won't *take long*' or 'This won't *hurt much*' or 'Don't be *scared*' (my italics). And, as we have seen, it plants in the patient's mind exactly the opposite of their intention.

Information as instructions

However precisely you say that you only want the train times, there is a risk that the person will over-deliver, as this over-response is often hard-wired (ie unchangeable) in them. So, use the pattern to break the pattern. Talk calmly with the person, during a calm moment, about their pattern of over-delivery. Let them know that their attitude is fabulous. (Do people still use that word, meaning literally the stuff of legend? I do, because that is precisely what this attitude is. Priceless.) Calmly inform them that no matter what they've been told by other people, in 21st-century organizations no one needs to be anxious to over-please, just to please enough. And, calmly, reassure them that it is perfectly safe for them to do this. And to trust you when you tell them this. And to check with other colleagues if they are in any doubt. And always, to reassure themselves, to check back with the order-giver: 'So, you only want train times? Not tickets?'

In this way, their instincts are respected and preserved. Their initiative is encouraged (because sometimes we might have forgotten that we needed train tickets too!). And the pattern is quietly modified, as they'll want to over-please you by adopting this new pattern.

Instructions as information

However much you precisely spell out what exactly you are wanting, there is still a tendency for the person to block out the instruction to do what you've asked. So, if spelling it out patiently has not worked, it's time to use the tried and tested opposite: a big, impatient bang or two.

It is useful, not to mention legally essential, to record the incidents in writing, for a formal performance appraisal. Compile a sheet that details all their successes, and then the categories of performance where you are looking for improvement. In each category, have three specific examples of non-performance or failure to achieve. Then you can fairly discuss with the person what exactly they need to be able to achieve in order to improve their performance to clearly specified standards within a specific time period.

This will go relatively smoothly, as the person will probably take this in as information, not instructions! And, of course, there will have been an area of discussion en route where they dispute that they failed on the specifics, and argue that maybe they weren't briefed clearly. (And this *may* be true; perhaps their manager hadn't had the time or ability to brief them effectively.)

Crucially – and this is Big Bang time – you need to discuss what exactly will happen if they do not meet the performance criteria agreed. Ask *them* for suggestions, because it's time that they switch from not having taken responsibility for their own actions, to taking responsibility. You may also ask them to come back to you later, having thought about it.

And – Big Bang Two – you could ask them what the whole pattern on the paper adds up to, in their opinion, and what, if they were you, they would do about it. Again, they may be rather stunned, having to think about it in this way, and may need time to think about it and allow it to sink in.

Whatever the outcomes, these two bangs should begin a process whereby they start seeing things differently and should enable them to realize what they need to *do* differently. And, naturally, some people may be devastated at seeing the reality of their actions or inactions in black and white like this, and may need considerable support, not to get back on track – because they were on the 'wrong' track – but to find new ways of working. After all, they may have upset a lot of people who will need to give them a second (at least) chance.

Disrespectful people

who may also be Belittlers, Dismissive, Flippant, Humiliators, Insensitive, Politically Incorrect and/or Put-Downers

What ticks us off

They make light of situations and shrug off their mistakes and responsibilities as if they don't matter. They disregard us and our opinions, and those of people close to us. It feels so belittling – how *dare* they!

How it can happen

They never seem to take anything seriously enough. Some demonstrate this with a gesture, like a dismissive wave of the hand, turning their back on us, or answering their phone while we're talking to them. Others throw out comments like 'Don't be stupid!' or 'Your friend is an [insult]!'

OK, some people *deliberately* put others down in order to try to make themselves appear superior (see chapter on Bullies). But many people disrespect others *unwittingly* as they genuinely fail to understand the seriousness of the situation.

We could speculate forever about how this might have come about. Some people might have been brought up not to 'worry their little head' about weighty matters. Others might have been told that 'it's nice to be able to lighten the mood with a joke to cheer people up' or 'don't take things too seriously' or 'don't take things to heart'.

But what they all have in common is that they make us feel disrespected, don't they? Wrong! Contrary to popular opinion, no one can *make* us feel anything. So when we hear people saying 'he made me so angry' or 'she really annoys me' or in this case 'they really made me feel small/belittled/humiliated/insignificant' – no, they didn't. We did that to ourselves. Not deliberately of course. No one deliberately wants to make themselves feel like a victim, do they? But feeling disrespected can really 'make' us feel (ie we can make ourselves feel) trapped. Shakespeare's Hamlet summed it up succinctly '... there is nothing either good or bad, but thinking makes it so. To me it is a prison.'

'... thinking makes it so'

Two Buddhist monks were crossing the river when they spotted a woman who had been swept downstream towards them. The older monk caught her in his arms and carried her safely to the river bank where they continued on their journey. After a few days the younger monk said to the older one 'I can't keep quiet on this any longer! We're Buddhist monks. You know we're not allowed to touch women. And you touched that woman!'

The older monk replied quietly 'Yes, I did. In fact I not only touched her, but I carried her. And I not only carried her, but I carried her for five whole minutes. But you've been carrying her for five whole days.'

It is said that being unrealistic is 'doing or saying the same thing but expecting a different result' so it's clearly unrealistic for us to try to deal with disrespectful behaviour by expecting them to magically change without clear direction and role modelling, It's down to us to communicate more clearly.

Tips for handling disrespectful people

Don't take it personally

Remember the Buddhist monks? It's down to us how we interpret things and how we carry those interpretations around with us. We can always remind ourselves that it was just a gesture or a comment, not an insult about who we are. We can then focus on 'so what exactly were they asking or saying?' and 'so what exactly am I going to do next?' or we could even do what many people do, and 'put it behind us'.

Putting it behind us

Some people literally put bad things behind them, instead of having them constantly 'in their face' or 'weighing on their mind'. They imagine sweeping them over their left shoulder (which seems the more effective shoulder for most people) with their right hand, and the bad things seem to fade away as they do it. They can still be used for learning from (eg asking how exactly did that 'make' me feel so bad?) without the negative feelings that were there when it was 'in their face' or 'on their mind'.

In my shoes

Since many people show disrespect unwittingly, we might try offering them some gentle guidance, eg 'Pat, if you were to put yourself in my shoes [and then maybe pause a little for this strange concept to sink in!] how do you think *I* felt when we were in the middle of our meeting and you turned your back on me to have a phone conversation with not so much as an 'excuse me'?'

Then allow time for Pat to consider this and if the silence becomes too long change the subject, eg 'Anyway, I've said my piece, thanks. See you later!'

Remember who did it to you first

It's worth thinking a little not just about what 'presses our button' but who first pressed it. For example, some of us react angrily if someone turns their back on us, or waves us away with the back of their hand across our eyes. They remind us of someone who really upset us, even though they are a different person in a different place and time. We need to realize this.

Point out the pattern

I'm a great believer in not trying to deal with a situation while it's actually happening. I find it much more effective (and calm) to point to a *series* of similar situations in a calm moment *between* situations. Why? Because there's enough to deal with when *in* a situation, let alone trying to deal with the pattern at the same time.

So I might explain that I was concerned that their responses had not been – in my opinion – appropriate. I'd quote examples (three is a good number to indicate the pattern without getting heavy handed). I'd explain that I took full responsibility myself for not being clear enough about the gravity of the situation, and about the precise type of responses that I should have asked for. I'd apologize for my lack of precision and clarity. And then I'd promise to be clearer in future, pause, and then change the subject to avoid a heavy silence hanging between us, waiting to be filled.

And as well as carefully choosing the time for this conversation, I'd carefully choose the place. Having it face to face across my desk, or standing over them while they're seated at theirs is much less effective for me than a chat in a more relaxed environment where the person can feel more open to consider what's being discussed.

Political correctness

Some words and phrases that were inoffensive when we were growing up might be considered offensive and disrespectful nowadays, and unless we know about them, we can unwittingly cause offence. The truth is that however sensitive we might try to be, we cannot know everyone's 'buttons' that will cause them to feel disrespected.

It may be sensible, therefore, eg in new situations or teams, to pass around a piece of paper for people to write down the words they feel are truly offensive to them, and for everyone to have a copy of this. After all, unless we actively find out, how else can we know other than by painful trial and error?

And it is vital – if we unwittingly disrespect someone – to apologize effectively. Short sentences, then a change of subject. For example, 'I'm sorry that what I said upset you. That was absolutely not my intention. I apologize unreservedly. Now, moving on to...'

Of course there might be some people who can't accept such a simple and truthful apology, and who want to make more of it. In truth, we can never know exactly what sort of apology might satisfy someone else – a hug? a written note? who knows? And so the answer is to ask them. 'What more do you want from me, then, by way of apology? Please let me know?' Then we can pause for them to think and if they can't think of anything we can simply change the subject, eg 'Let me know later if you like. Meanwhile, is everyone OK if we move on to...?'

16

Dumpers

who may mistakenly believe they are Delegators

What ticks us off

Everyone agrees that delegating is an essential part of managing and leading. But too often the delegatee feels dumped upon. And more often than not, the delegator feels – usually quite rightly! – that it would be quicker to do it themselves than to delegate.

How it can happen

It's a real Catch-22. If there's enough time for us to do a task, we'll tend to do it ourselves. Because we can. And because it's easier, quicker and safer to keep control of it.

If there is *not* enough time for us to do a task, we tend to end up 'dumping' on someone else, whether or not we dress it up and call it 'delegating' or even an 'opportunity' or a 'challenge'. Why? Because there is simply not enough time to 'delegate' the task properly. We end up by frustrating everyone involved!

And another thing. Sometimes, frustratingly, the person who is delegating will cause great confusion by telling someone not only *what* to do, but *how* to do it – all jumbled up together.

So, delegation is much admired, applauded and encouraged, but it is less often done effectively.

Tips for handling dumpers

The key to delegating is to understand that – because of the dumping and doing-it-yourself tendencies referred to above – it only really works when we delegate a *type* of task, not an individual task. And delegating a *type* of task means that the delegatee can handle a whole category of tasks, not just the one. And in this way, they have been trained. And developed. Because they can genuinely deputize for the delegator, long term.

This means taking time to delegate properly – not when there's an urgent task to be done!

When being dumped on

Here's a simple, effective delegation model. Hand it to the dumper.

1. Plan who to delegate to, how long it will take to delegate (ie coach, teach, train) properly, and when and where and how it would be best to do it.
2. Explain exactly *what* is needed (not *how* to do it, yet), in what form, for what purpose, and when.
3. Invite delegatee/deputy to respond, after thinking, by confirming what the brief is.
4. Clarify the brief, if necessary, eg:
   - 'What you correctly understood is…'
   - 'What you added in, that I did not specify, is…'
   - 'What you left out is…' Repeat 2 and 3 if necessary.
5. Invite delegatee to consider:
   - how they might achieve this;
   - what resources/training they'll need;
   - what support/supervision they want;
   - what authority they'll need;
   - who else needs to be informed that they have this authority.

6. Negotiate on the reassurances that you both want, that the project is going to be on track.
7. And on completion discuss:
   - feedback;
   - feedforward; and
   - learnings for each of you – on the specific project and category.

17

Embarrassed people

who may also Belittle Themselves and/or their Achievements, or be Excessively Modest or Quiet, Reluctant to Accept Praise/Compliments, Scared to Speak Up, Self-deprecating, Self-effacing, Shy

What ticks us off

It's infuriating, if not ridiculous, when we praise or congratulate someone for what they've done, and they blushingly say 'It was nothing' or they point out the mistakes they'd made that we hadn't noticed!

'Just say yes'

A few years ago a client from the United States congratulated me on some work I had done, and as I was going through the routine of 'Oh, it wasn't so difficult, and I was in the area anyway, and blah blah blah...' he exploded at me. 'You Brits!!! When someone pays you a compliment why do you have to be so defensive? Why can't you just say "thank you" instead of going on and on belittling yourself, and your achievement, and our opinion of you? It's as though you're telling us that our opinion of you is wrong!'

And he threw lots of other examples my way: if we're told we have a nice tie, we'll explain that we got it in a sale, or it has a loose thread – and so on!

How it can happen

Often, people can feel embarrassed if 'they' are paid a compliment. (Not their behaviour, but them as a person.) For example (and there's usually an audibly gushing exclamation mark attached):

- 'You *are* clever!'
- 'What a good child you've been!'
- 'What a great presenter you are!'

However flattering this may be, it's absolutely useless as praise, because the person doesn't have a clue as to what exactly they said or did that was appreciated. What else to do in this situation but blush and mumble?

Also, many people simply do not know how to respond to genuine praise (and maybe it's also because praise is relatively uncommon, especially in 'blame' cultures?). They feel embarrassed by the silence that follows a compliment, and they need to fill the silence, and keep on filling it, not knowing how or when to stop.

✓ TIP

Tips for handling embarrassed people

Get it straight

If they've become embarrassed because the praise has been gushing but unspecific, point this out to them and encourage them to get clarification so that they know what exactly to keep doing! For example:

- 'You said "You are clever!", and I'd love to know what exactly I did or said, please?'
- 'When you said "What a good child you've been!", what exactly did you mean, please?'

■ 'When you told me "What a great presenter you are!",
  what specifically did you have in mind, please?'

(And, of course, *you* always give specific and behavioural
praise, to avoid the problem in the first place, don't you?!)

Thank you

After you know what you've been praised for, just say 'thank
you' or 'thank you very much' and then *change the subject*. For
example:

■ 'Thank you. Now the next item on the agenda is...'; or
■ 'Thank you very much – you presented very clearly yourself! Now shall we move on to... '

Why change the subject? To avoid that embarrassed silence.

18

Forgetful people

who may also be prone to Losing Things

What ticks us off

Some people are 'always' losing things, or forgetting things. Keys? Deadlines? Birthdays? And while the effect of some of these can be relatively trivial, others can be enormous (eg forgetting your passport, or your boss's requests). And it can be very, very annoying for colleagues and friends.

How it can happen

Some people don't remember (or, more accurately, re-remember) things simply because they were not significant at the time, or because they were not alerted to the fact that they 'should' need to re-member them sometime in the future. For example, if I asked you exactly how much small change you had exactly 35 days ago, you probably wouldn't have a clue, and why should you? But if I asked you to count the money you have on you today, you'd be better organized to re-remember it at some time in the future.

Other people take time to remember things ('It's on the tip of my tongue!') and know that they know the information, but don't have it immediately 'to hand'.

Tips for handling forgetful people

Look left

Most people think of their past memories on their left-hand side and their future plans on their right. So, if you're trying to help someone remember something, encourage them to 'look' out for the image, or 'listen' again for it, to their left.

Call first, then re-call

Encourage forgetful people to take a mental snapshot. If you don't have a piece of information in the first place, then it's impossible to recall it! Keys are a good example. If you put them down wherever you happen to put them down, where can you look for them? Only where you've put them (and therefore found them) in the past. Not where you put them (and haven't yet found them!) today. So, if the person's keys don't have their own place, suggest that they take a mental snapshot of them as, and immediately after, they put them down. And to make it easier, ask them to think something like 'Keys thrown into left shoe by front door'. Or, to make it even easier still, ask them to say it aloud so they can re-remember hearing themselves saying it, *and* remember thinking it, *and* remember seeing it in their mental snapshot.

'Over the shoulder'

I often used to 'lose' my car in car parks. A friend of mine, however, was like a homing pigeon – arriving directly at his car first time, every time. So I watched how he did it. The trick was that a few steps after leaving his car in the first place, he'd look over his left (note, left!) shoulder and take a quick mental snapshot of it. And he'd do the same again at every turn of our walk. So, to find it he just had to re-call these images in reverse order. Simple when you know how, and reassuring that those of us who had not been doing this didn't have anything wrong with us. We weren't genetically incapable of finding our car; we just hadn't learnt how to find it.

Everything in its place

Back to those keys, if they could only find them! A simple strategy is to allocate a place for everything. Without that place, there can be much fruitless searching, without a map.

Encourage forgetful people to adopt the following additional strategies

Re-minding ourselves

The more often we re-mind ourselves, the easier it is to re-call the information, because the best way of remembering something is to re-visit it several times to help it 'stick'.

For example, if I asked you to think of your favourite or worst teacher, you could probably re-call their face and/or name and/or voice quite easily, even if you hadn't thought of them for quite some time. Because you saw them, initially at least, frequently.

In this way, we can give ourselves an excellent chance of re-calling something we've just done if we re-visit it briefly the next day, again a week later, and maybe a month after that – for shorter times each time.

3D or 5D memories?

If we take a mental snapshot (1) of where we threw (2) our keys, and say it (3) out loud at the same time, that gives us three senses for re-calling it. If we'd added 'in that smelly left shoe (4) by the creaking (5) front door', we'd be adding two more senses and so be stacking the odds in favour of re-remembering the location.

The more multi-sensory the memory, the more ways there are to re-remember it. (And if we actually put up a solid key hook in an easy location and then use it, well – that's going to work automatically without our even having to think about it!)

Name names

There are people who complain that they can never remember people's names. In fact, that used to be me, until I learnt that for people who are not very visual, remembering names can be quite a challenge.

The best strategy I've come across so far is to imagine the person's name written on their forehead, while their mouth tells me their name and with their hairstyle and clothes constantly changing! (This is to ensure that in the likely event that they *do* ever change their hairstyle or clothes, my memory of their name will be unchanged.)

So, when someone tells you their name, imagine their mouth repeatedly pronouncing it, and see it written on their forehead while you play with the typeface and colour of the letters to make it as appropriate as possible. For example, if I meet someone from Germany, I might use an old German typeface. Or if I meet someone who's a musician, I might make the letters like musical notes.

And to increase the chances of remembering the name, try to increase the number of senses involved. So, as well as *seeing* the name, you might also *say* it to yourself a few times, and possibly *write* it invisibly on your leg or in your pocket with a finger.

Another variation is to pop on their shoulder any object that might you help to remember *where* you met them, so a little Eiffel Tower might be perched on one shoulder and their company logo on another.

It's fun to have fun with this, because all these decisions you are making about *how* exactly to remember a specific name (typeface, colour, objects on shoulders, etc) will help to fix it in your memory.

Don't forget

When we say 'I must not forget…', we very often do forget! It's much more effective to say, or think of, what we *do* want to do (eg 'I must remember that I threw my keys into that smelly left shoe…') than to say or think of what we don't want.

19

Gossipy people

who may also be Cliquey and Rumour-mongers

What ticks us off

There they are in a huddle again – I wonder who they're talking about this time? I hope they're not talking about me! Oh no, I think they are – they keep looking in my direction. I feel so insecure and helpless and powerless and excluded and victimized and paranoid. Or maybe they're talking about my colleague again? I'm sure they've got it in for them. What on earth can I do?

How it can happen

Gossip is all around us, though it is sometimes called conversation or small talk or news. Look at all the celebrity magazines we (all right, other people) buy. Look at all the paparazzi, journalists and news editors we indirectly employ to feed us the gossip that fills the media day after day, week after week. Look at how many people want to look big in other people's eyes, by making others look small. Look at how gossip fills a vacuum of facts, and creates suspicion and a 'them and us' atmosphere.

Tips for handling gossipy people

Coffee time

In organizations – including families and groups of friends – people form alliances and allegiances which can become gossipy cliques with soft voices and harsh laughter. They meet up and chat, eg 'What do you think about what Pat said in that meeting yesterday?' or 'Have you heard about the redundancies?'

We must realize that if we're not in this group then there's little we can do about it, and any attempt to break into it is likely to backfire, because they've already chosen their members and we're not one of them.

But some time *afterwards* it could be productive for us to find something to talk about with two or three of the individuals in the group, separately though. So at least we'll know that we've begun to sow seeds in their minds of 'well maybe they're OK… I had a conversation with them about X'. Or at least we can *imagine* that this is what they'll be saying, instead of imagining what we'd been imagining before!

A content loner

Following on from this, it can do no harm to turn our exclusion from the clique to our advantage. We can reframe it as eg 'I know I don't take part in many group things, but I'm a bit of a loner – and that's just my way. It's not a reflection on anyone else of course. You do understand, don't you?' In this way we can position our 'outsider' status as our own decision, and not theirs. Again, it helps us to feel more in control, and in truth we are, since we've taken this initiative.

Facts or no facts

It's vital for us to spread facts before others spread rumours.

For example, if we're planning to make some posts redundant, or reorganize some departments, or promote or demote someone, then we must say so! And we must say it as soon as we can, and make sure that we say it clearly, honestly and comprehensively, leaving no gaps for people to fill in for themselves. Because people who suspect something will anxiously be trying to protect their own position, and morale will suffer, work will suffer and probably even home lives will suffer. And we're only kidding ourselves if we think that information will never leak out – it's like water and will leak out from the most unexpected places.

Similarly, if we're honestly *not* planning to do something we should say so as well, eg 'there is a rumour that we are about to do X. Well I assure you that it's an unfounded rumour and not to be trusted, and if you want any further reassurance please come to me and ignore the rumour-mongers.' And it does no harm at all to state that there is a rumour-monger, or at least to spread it as a rumour in this way: they'll feel discovered and somewhat exposed and may even lie low for a while.

Deliberately floating positive rumours

If we're thinking about doing something in our team or organization and we're not sure if it's a good idea, we might float the idea with some people and ask them to let us know what they think about it. If it is a good idea, then the people we've asked will have done the pre-selling for us. If it's not a good idea, we'll save ourselves a lot of time and trouble. And if there are changes needed then we need to listen! And in the process we'll get the reputation of someone who's confident enough to talk openly and honestly with other people and – even more importantly – to listen and accept 'advice'.

A friend of mine, incidentally, had what he thought was a great way of doing this. He used to send out an e-mail to float an idea, then send out another to 'recall' it, and see what people said when he asked them about the idea anyway. He'd tell people 'I'm not asking everyone about this, of course, but

I'd really value your opinion' and then he'd ask everyone, and ask them not to tell anyone that they'd had this conversation. So they felt special, and he got lots of feedback. But of course this works only once, or people will know that it is a ploy.

Similarly, I've known people who will put a notice on a notice board, and when two or three people have seen it, they will take it down again. This raises speculation not only about what was in the notice, but why it was removed so quickly. I don't recommend these e-mail or notice board ploys as open, honest, transparent, or anything else that we'd like our organization to be!

'Flush them out'

Shortly after I was made a director I got a new office and a damp patch on the carpet. The radiator was leaking, so I rang Sid, who came up, inspected it, and told me that I had a leak in my radiator, and that he'd order me a new one. He emptied it out and left it propped against the wall. Naturally, most people who spotted it asked 'what's wrong with your radiator?', which has always struck me as a pointless question unless you've run out of small talk and need to resort to very small talk! Well, as it happens, there was another leak in the department. We knew that someone had been spreading rumours and leaking information and we hadn't been able to find out who it was. So when people were enquiring about the health of my radiator I decided to give different answers to different people. 'It's ridiculous isn't it, but when you're made a director you get a new radiator upgrade!' or 'Apparently, they need to be rested from time to time, otherwise they can get blocked.' You get the idea. So when the 'new director = new radiator' story came back to me ('Is it *really* true, Mike, that you get a new radiator when you're made a director?') I knew who'd spread it around, and told them that actually there was a leak in the department of a more serious nature and I was planning to deal with that one too. Of course I've no idea whether the radiator leaker was the information leaker, but the word got around all the same and the information leak stopped.

'Glasgow's much better these days'

So said a friend of mine, who invited me for the weekend. She guided me around the Cathedral with the comic-book stained glass. She showed me the Charles Rennie Mackintosh architecture. I was having a great time. Until I picked up my phone messages. There were 11. All from my boss, my boss's boss and my boss's boss's boss. 'Mike, could you give me a call please?' 'Mike, I need to speak to you urgently.' 'Mike, please ring me immediately about this Hot News in Marketing Week.' And so on.

I rang a friend, who read the article to me. It explained that I was rumoured to be taking a top job with a competing advertising agency. (This was untrue – I was talking to their parent company about an even topper job!) So I rang my boss and was able – honestly – to deny the rumour. But, boy, did I feel insecure, helpless, powerless, excluded, victimized and paranoid! Who had spread this rumour and why had they done it? And – uselessly, because I knew it was impossible – how could I undo the suspicion and lack of trust that this had spread?

And, since you ask, I later found out that a colleague of mine had been going for that top job (not the topper job – hah!) and he was feeling insecure as he thought he'd be competing with me, or worse still have to report to me, and so he wanted to sabotage my chances. What did I do about this? I didn't want to make it into anything more complicated than it was already, so I did absolutely nothing, and it gradually faded away, although these things can never fade away completely, can they? And luckily, I chose not to leave my job, so my continued presence was something of a reassurance, even when the rumour-monger announced that he'd got his new job. And I was able to say, honestly, that I hoped it was worth all the effort he'd put into getting it, and then winked at him.

20

Hostile people

who may also appear to be Alienating,
Antagonistic, Argumentative, Confrontational,
Disaffected, Disloyal, Disrespectful, Grudging,
Obstructive, Resentful, Ridiculing, Rude, Sarcastic,
Snide, Sulky, Trouble-makers, Uncooperative,
Undermining, Unforgiving, Unfriendly, Vengeful
or Vindictive

What ticks us off

There are so many forms of hostility ranging from calculated coolness through unfriendliness to downright rudeness. It can spread from one person to create 'an atmosphere' in a whole team or department such that absenteeism rises along with staff turnover, because people – sensibly – don't want to work 'here'. It's not conducive to a good atmosphere, it's pretty unpleasant personally and it's easy to fix.

How it can happen

When people mutter, glower, grunt, snap, sneer, blank us completely or give us the cold shoulder, it's pretty clear that:

■ something's on their mind;
■ it's not a good something; and
■ it involves us somehow.

There are many, many individual reasons why this arises, and they tend to cluster into a few clear patterns.

Grudges

Bearing grudges involves bringing the bad feelings from a past event or series of events into the present and letting them affect current behaviours. Often the person carries in their mind's eye a vivid picture of the original unfair or unjust behaviour(s), and this clouds their judgement. They continue to treat the person or situation as they experienced them in the past, even though the current circumstances may have moved on significantly.

Generalization

Generalization can happen where a *specific* problem event happened, and yet the person reacts in a hostile way not only to those involved with the original event, but to lots of other things and people around them. You can feel like saying, 'Hang on! It wasn't me who did that, so why are you getting at me?'

'Get straight to the point'

In a team I was training, I noticed that one person was constantly picking on everything I said, making snide remarks to his colleagues and generally enabling me to interpret his behaviour as 'hostile' to me. I hypothesized that either I'd been doing a pretty bad job for him, or something was being generalized in my direction. I chose to have a quiet word at the first break, rather than deal with it with the rest of the team as spectators! Following the 1–4 structure explained on page 82 (instinctively, I realize), I said quietly, 'I notice, John [let's call him], that you've been picking me up on most of what I've said, and that makes me feel that I'm not meeting your needs here. Because I want to feel useful to you, tell me if it's what I'm doing, or if it's something personal between us, or what I can do differently to meet your needs better.'

He looked horrified; his face fell, and he gushed out an apology. There was a close relative of his, close to death, and he'd rather have been with his family at that moment than in my training group. We talked a little about this, and how his boss had decided that he'd be better off at work to keep his mind off 'the situation' – as if that were wholly possible in the circumstances! So we agreed that he could keep his phone on, in case he was needed. And we changed the seating so that he could sit near the back and make a quick exit if he needed to, without having to excuse himself too publicly. And we agreed that if he just needed to go for a walk, or a break, that was fine too.

And, finally, we agreed on a form of words for informing the rest of the team of these 'exceptions' to the rules (mobile phones, leaving the group, etc), and became close friends thereafter, all from a supposedly 'hostile' beginning.

Inferiority complexes

Individuals with inferiority complexes have beliefs such as 'They are better than me' and 'I'm bound to be found out soon, so I'd better keep people away from me, using hostility.' They may have a chip on their shoulder, for whatever reason, and can get defensive or aggressive/defensive as a result.

This fear of being 'found out' is also – perhaps not surprisingly – quite common among people at senior levels who have recently been promoted.

'Mind the gap'

I remember a person in a senior position being interviewed on television, and at the end of the interview he confided to the camera 'You know the cause of most of the stress in people at senior levels in organizations? We have *huge* egos and, in truth, *tiny* self-esteem!'

Energy

When people rarely use much physical energy, they may simply need to get their energy levels up – to feel 'alive' – through, for example, having heated arguments whenever they can.

Tips for handling hostile people

If someone has a powerful need for this hostile type of energy, it can easily cloud their awareness of the consequences if they haven't stopped to think of the effect that they are having on other people.

This is reasonably easy to bring to their attention, with a suggestion that they find other, less damaging ways of communicating, ways that are still effective but without the undesired hurt. (These people can often be upset or even devastated that they either hadn't considered or hadn't noticed the consequences of their actions. They may need reassurance that this hurtful behaviour of theirs obviously wasn't deliberate on their part.)

Calibrate, then modulate

Lack of calibration of, for example, their volume and intensity might mean that they *think* they are 'acting normally'. A quiet word of advice is for them to notice the volume and intensity that they use, and to notice the levels generally used by other people. This might well do the trick. After all, hostility was never intended – only perceived.

Have you ever experienced the serving staff in Manhattan's bars and restaurants? You might think that 'Waddywan?' or 'Wocnigecha?' is loud, rude, abrupt and lacking in all the social niceties, but their intention is to be efficient, serve you quickly and get a big tip for doing so! This is 'normal' behaviour in these environments, and is not intended to be hostile. Similarly, acting 'normally' in a big, busy, noisy household might mean shouting to be heard, and acting quickly to avoid being left out. The same behaviours in a workplace can, however, be interpreted as hostile because of the alienating effects on all concerned.

Get below the hostility

Asking 'what's wrong with *you?*' or 'what's the matter with *you?*' can backfire, sometimes dramatically, with a useless response such as 'You should know!' or 'Well, if you can't remember, it's obviously not important to you!' or 'There's nothing wrong with *me!*' And all of this makes perfect sense when you realize that they are reliving a vivid picture of how they were hurt.

'Is anything the matter?' can get a similar response, but, being a closed question, will get a curter response such as 'No' or 'You should know.' Or similar.

Take responsibility, therefore, for wanting to put things right and move the situation forward, without blaming or digging up past hurts. A useful structure is:

1. what I noticed;
2. what I felt as a result;
3. what needs I have that are not yet met;
4. what request I'm making, as a consequence.

And remember, it is what *you* notice, feel, need and want – not pointing the finger and telling the other person what *they* were feeling, or needing. That can be very intrusive and counterproductive; just think of a time when someone said to you, 'You must be feeling very X' – and you weren't!

EXAMPLES

Help me to help you

'I notice that you've been loud and abrupt in my direction recently and I'm feeling a bit anxious as a result, because I need to keep this team – including yourself – on target. So can I ask you to tell me what exactly I need to do differently for you?'

And then, importantly, leave a silence. This type of question needs to be translated and internalized (as, say, '... what exactly *do* you need to do differently for me?') before they can then begin to answer it.

After *too* long a silence, though, you might suggest that they may want to consider it further and meet up later – at 5 pm, in the morning at 9 am, or at another specific time and place.

We've been talking about you...

'We've noticed that you've been quieter and not mixing with the team recently and because I am concerned about every single member of the team, I need to know what I need to do, please?'

(If the 'we've noticed...' gets a hostile reaction, such as 'So you've all been talking about me behind my back, have you?', it's perfectly safe to be honest, along the lines of 1–4 in the list above. For example: 'Of course we have, as we felt concerned for you as a member of our team, and we want and need to know how we can help, so maybe we can talk about it – now or after work – please?'

'You can't contradict me, Mr Leibling'

After school, when I was working in Lilley & Skinner, the shoe shop, in Western Road, Brighton, I contradicted something that Mr Nicholls, the manager, had just said to me.

'Mr Leibling,' he said, in his kindly voice, 'you can't contradict what I just said.'

'Sorry, Mr Nicholls,' I muttered, thinking he meant that this was because he was the manager and I was very junior (all right, *the* junior!).

'Aren't you going to ask why you can't contradict what I just said, Mr Leibling?' he asked gently. 'Sorry, Mr Nicholls,' I muttered again. 'Why can't I contradict you?'

'Because, Mr Leibling, I began my sentence with "I think". When someone says something like "I think..." or "I feel..." or "I believe..." or "I want...", how can anyone tell them that they *don't* think or feel or believe or want whatever it is?'

21

Impatient people

who may also be Complainers, Intolerant and Unreasonable

What ticks us off

Impatient people just can't wait. Everything is done too slowly, and takes too long, except when they do things themselves.

How it can happen

Sometimes these people don't have a clue as to how long things really take, and therefore have unrealistic expectations (after all, we can only be disappointed if we first have expectations).

Sometimes they leave things until the very last minute, possibly because they themselves are dumped upon, or possibly because they simply do not plan ahead. Sometimes also they have a very fixed idea of *how* they want the job done and expect other people to follow the same path, even if there are better/cheaper/easier/faster paths that the person could take to the required destination.

It's also common that some people feel that it is their duty to bully people by giving them too little time to do the job properly, and that these people should work all possible hours to serve them!

Tips for handling impatient people

There are many ways to address someone's impatience, preferably not when the person is jumping up and down, but in a quiet moment.

Panics? What panics?

Many people tend to have urgent panics on Friday afternoons, especially just before a vacation of theirs (or mine), or at a public holiday weekend. Since they've not been very good at planning ahead, try ringing them a few days beforehand and asking what they'll be needing from you. Or what their boss, in turn, will be asking of them.

We'd love your advice, please

Under the guise of wanting their expert advice, you might invite them to shadow you, or accompany you to whoever actually *does* what they need, so that they can see, hear and feel the reality of what they have asked for.

You can ask for any advice they might have that would speed the process, and they might well have some. You will also be able to allow them to experience the reality of what they've asked for. And, in future panics, you can explain how they know from their experience what needs to happen, and ask them to choose which corners to cut, or to ease the deadline.

What, how?

I always try to unpick *what* I've been asked to do from *how* it's been suggested that I do it. After all:

- ■ I may not be able to do it as suggested
- ■ and it might take longer
- ■ and be more expensive

■ and less satisfying
■ and, therefore, it might turn out to be a significantly less successful way of achieving the *what* than using my own skills and preferences (assuming that there are no specific health and/or safety requirements that must be satisfied).

So, typically:

1. I will check back on what exactly I understand their need to be, including when and where and in what form they want it delivered.
2. I will then say that they asked me to do it in a specific way and ask if they are happy for me to do it a different way (and describe that to them, if it makes them or me comfortable to do so).

Discounts

Many people seem to get enormous pleasure from piling on the deadline pressure but resent paying for it, refusing to pay for 'rush' charges, overtime or subcontracting, for example.

I offer *discounts*, therefore – for example: 'Yes, that can certainly be achieved by X pm today. However, after looking into it, we could save you Y per cent of the cost if it's ready by 9 am tomorrow, or Y + Z per cent if it's ready by X pm tomorrow.' (And then this is the crucial bit...) 'Which do you prefer?' (And naturally the 'rush' charges, overtime or subcontracting would be calculated into the base cost to which the discounts can be applied, because that's the reality, isn't it?)

Bully for you

If the person likes to wield power and bully, I'm happy to play along with it a little, but with a tiny twinkle in my eye, and the full knowledge that I'm not suffering, or feeling genuinely bullied.

So maybe you could use phrases to flatter their sense of self such as:

■ 'Well, since you drive such a hard bargain...'
■ 'Well, seeing that it's you...'
■ 'We couldn't do this for everyone, but...'

in the full knowledge that this makes them feel good, does you no harm, and they are paying for it in any case!

22

Impetuous, impulsive people

What ticks us off

Some people blurt out the first thing that comes to their mind, often without hearing the whole of what is needed. Others can leap into action while they are still being briefed, or without considering the implications of what they are doing. They may think that they are quick and efficient, but often what they say or do needs to be undone and then redone – and they'll often blame others for having briefed them incorrectly, or for having changed their mind about what they wanted, whereas in reality they hadn't waited for the whole picture before leaping into action.

How it can happen

Frequently, a pattern of impetuous, impulsive behaviour goes back to a common but misplaced desire to get 1) the 'right' answer 2) quickly. This can stem from school, where being the first to get your hand up and getting the answer right was highly praised by some misguided teachers. Why misguided? Well, because all the children who were slower, more thorough thinkers didn't really stand a chance in this type of showy display. Also, it led to the impression that the first answer was more prized than the thought-through answer.

Tips for handling impetuous, impulsive people

Think it through, please

If you want a considered approach from someone else, try spelling out not only what you want, but also how you want them to approach it – for example: 'Before you respond/act I'd like a short memo covering all the options you can think of, and the consequences/risks/benefits of each option in the short, medium and long term, please.' (Writing the options in a memo will force them to think more. If it doesn't, use more words and phrases such as 'considered' or 'thought-through' or 'thorough' or 'that you're prepared to stake your reputation on' and give them at least overnight to think about the question. If they give it to you much sooner, tell them that you don't feel they could have considered it enough yet in the short time that they've had, and that you value their full consideration of all the issues.)

Think about what you're asking me

If someone is pressuring you for an instant response and you're not comfortable, or able or prepared to give one, try getting them to think of the consequences of what they're asking you to achieve – for example: 'I'm happy to give you right now the first answers that come to my mind, or more considered ones in an hour's time, or some seriously thought-through ones in the morning. Which do you want?' This response then lets *them* decide, since it was they who had the urgency that they thrust at you.

Address the pattern

In a quiet moment you can usefully address this pattern of behaviour with the person who has been exhibiting it – for example: 'You've always been brilliant at leaping into action, and less thorough in thinking things through, so we've often had to redo your work, or ask you to redo it.' (And have a few recent examples to hand, in case they look bemused.) 'What do we need to do to help you to take a more thorough approach to your work?'

Or 'You've been asking for lots of snap decisions from me recently' (again, have a few recent examples to hand, in case they look bemused) 'which I've been happy to give you, but I'd much rather give you properly thought-through decisions or maybe even some options for us to discuss. How can we improve the quality of our recommendations?' (And you might want a few suggestions up your sleeve, for them to take away and consider, rather than impetuously agree upon, on the spot!) 'For example, maybe you could involve me at the same time that you yourself get involved? Perhaps you could direct them to me in the first place, to save time? Maybe you can just make the decision yourself, and don't feel you have to keep me in the loop?'

23

Indecisive people

who generally Find It Hard to Make Decisions

What ticks us off

It can be intensely frustrating if we are expecting or needing decisions from someone and all we get is 'I don't know, really, I'm not sure' or 'Do I have to decide now?' or 'Why don't you decide?' or 'I really can't decide.' Not to mention the frustration that they themselves feel.

Easy decisions are called no-brainers. Tough ones hurt our brains!

How it can happen

There are *many* possible patterns, and tips for dealing with them.

Don't want

Some people are better at knowing what they *don't* want than what they do want.

A tip for handling indecisive people who are better at knowing what they *don't* want

Eliminate

Ask them what they don't want, and what else they don't want, until they've exhausted their list. Then maybe you and they together can be curious about what options are left. And don't ever seriously expect them to sound enthusiastic. The best you will get – in keeping with this decision style – is something like 'Well, I suppose there's no harm in going with that one' or 'I can't see why not.'

Here's an example that may seem very simple, but the last step is vital and often left out!

1. Draw up a checklist of criteria with them, for making the decision.
2. Apply weightings.
3. Score each option.
4. Allow the decision-maker to decide *against* the leading options!

As an example, to decide which of several sites is best for your new premises, you might list as criteria:

■ accessibility to current staff;
■ good local workforce available;
■ appealing location and/or facilities, eg shops;
■ value for money;
■ etc.

Then you would assign weightings to each, eg:

■ accessibility to current staff (7 out of 10 for importance);
■ good local workforce available (8);
■ appealing location and/or facilities, eg shops (5);
■ value for money (8).

Then you'd rate or assign marks out of 10 for each option:

- accessibility to current staff (3);
- good local workforce available (3);
- appealing location and/or facilities, eg shops (2);
- value for money (10).

Then, next to last, you'd multiply each site's marks against the weighting, add them up, and see which had the highest score.

And lastly, you'd allow the person who needs to decide, to react *against* the winner(s) – because that's their decision style! In this way you can continue to eliminate options until there's only one left.

Overloaded

Some people can't decide because there are too many factors to consider easily, and they feel overloaded or overwhelmed. It's like having too many pieces from too many jigsaw puzzles, all together. And this can feel very stressful.

A tip for handling indecisive people who feel overloaded

Indecision

This is a good tip for overloaded people who can't make decisions. In my experience, you cannot force an important decision; it makes itself, when it is good and ready. Hence, if we force a decision, when something later goes wrong we often say, for example, 'Do you know, I had a funny feeling at the time that this would go wrong.' That was our 'instinct' or 'gut feel' reacting against our forced so-called 'decision'.

So how does this help? Well, if a decision truly makes itself (or some people say that it makes itself *felt*) and it hasn't done so yet, then that is often because it needs to be fuelled with more information in order for a truly informed decision to be made, rather than an ill-informed one that 'feels wrong'.

What to do, then? Simple. Ask yourself, 'So what do I need right now? What am I missing or lacking in order to inform this decision?' Even better, ask someone else to ask you this (or imagine someone else asking you this) and make sure they don't stop asking 'What else...?' until you've thought of everything that you were missing. And you may not need to do this all at once, as you may benefit from sleeping on it.

Once all the relevant information is to hand, the decision will make itself, and make itself known to you, quickly. (After all, that's how *easy* decisions happen – with all the information to hand they make themselves, and make themselves known to us. We don't have to think about them. That's why we call them 'no-brainers'.)

Dilemmas

You know what they say:

- Having only one choice is a 'compulsion',
- two is a 'dilemma',
- but with three or more appealing options, we can begin to think and choose for real.

Being compelled to choose the *only* option can feel very pressured. People often feel tight in the chest as they feel they 'should' or 'have to' do what seems to be the only option. They feel 'under pressure' to do this. Take it or leave it. You have no choice.

So, you'd think that it would be better to have two choices, but choosing either one of the two unappealing options in a dilemma will also rarely lead to in a satisfactory result.

It's pretty well essential, therefore, to have at least three appealing options to choose from.

✓ TIP

A tip for handling indecisive people who are stuck in a dilemma

More options, please

If a person is stuck with only one option, offer them half a dozen 'maybes' or 'perhapses' to get their own thoughts going. (I've found that half a dozen opens up their thinking without leading them in a specific direction – especially if a few daft ones are thrown in, because you never know what might spark off appealing options for them.) For example, if they don't know whether to accept a dinner offer from their boss:

■ 'Maybe you could ask what the purpose is…?'
■ 'Perhaps you could find out who else will be there…?'
■ 'Perhaps you could ask what their ulterior motive is?!'
■ 'Maybe you could say you feel uncomfortable about meeting over dinner…?'
■ 'Maybe you could ask if it's for business or pleasure…?'
■ 'Perhaps you could ask if partners are invited too…?'

If someone is 'on the horns of a dilemma', the above process can help. So can constructing a third option by asking 'How about if you did both things, or neither?' For example, if they don't know whether to go to dinner with their boss, or to their child's parents' evening:

■ 'Maybe you could do *both* – and suggest a different time or day to your boss…?'
■ 'Perhaps there's a third option of doing *neither* – do you really want to go to the dinner or the parents' evening?'

And if they still can't think of any more appealing options:

■ 'Maybe you could sleep on it?'
■ 'Perhaps you could think what your favourite aunt/uncle/ mentor/friend might suggest?'

■ 'Maybe you could tell me what advice you'd really like me to give you?!' (And don't be tempted to give them any advice. It's their problem to solve, and they simply need to fuel it with more and more information until the decision makes itself.)

Where is that decision?

1. Internal

Some people tend to make decisions internally and call it 'gut feel' or 'intuition'. The rest of us might find it hard to understand why they've made this decision, because they find it even harder to explain – for example: 'I can't explain; I just know/feel/sense that it's right.' Asking 'Why?' seems to get us nowhere, often getting just a one-word reply, 'Because.' At other times, asking 'Why?' seems to freeze the person or conversation into a sudden silence. However kindly we meant it, it can be received by some people as a disbelieving challenge.

A tip for handling indecisive people who make decisions *internally*

Try how

It can be useful for the person who judges internally to develop their thinking externally, so that they can explain their reasoning to other people. Thus, questions like 'How exactly will the rest of us fit into that idea?' or 'How, precisely, would you see that working out longer term?' can help them to verbalize.

Of course, they *haven't* thought it through yet, so they'll need some time to 'think aloud' or go away and consider it. Maybe you could also focus their mind by asking them to jot down something in writing, too?

Where is that decision?

2. External

Some people don't actually seem not to make decisions; they collect data externally, and then make an impersonal pronouncement – for example: 'Having looked at the data, the obvious course to take is X' or 'I've spoken to a few people about this, and we'll be doing Y.' It'll be almost impossible to get them to say how they themselves feel about the situation or the decision, because they simply don't feel anything about it.

 ✓ TIP

A tip for handling indecisive people who make decisions *externally*

Keep cool

Value these people for their relative objectivity. They won't be comfortable if you put them (as a person with feelings) on the spot. Ask for their (external) view on a situation, not their (internal) feelings about it.

Insecure people

*who may also be Fragile, Intraverted, Loners,
Needing Constant Reassurance, Over-sensitive, Shy,
Thin-skinned, Timid, Unconfident, Victim-like, with
Low Confidence, Low Self-esteem, Low Self-worth*

What ticks us off

With some people we can feel we're always 'treading on eggshells'. We have to 'watch our step' and 'mind our tongue' in case we 'set them off' or 'upset them'. This can be quite a strain to handle in teams. It often happens, by the way, that the people concerned will have coping strategies such as bluffing, 'Yes, that's fine', coupled with a give-away glazed look in the eyes as they are panicking inside. (The glazed eyes, incidentally, are the result of their being focused solely on one thing: appearing confident, or in control, or not panicking. The eyes of someone who's thinking fluidly flicker and blink naturally.)

But – whatever the situation – they can get very hurt very easily, which is naturally best avoided.

How it can happen

On a relatively practical level, maybe they're worried about something, or about many things. This can, naturally, divert attention *inwards* and limit the amount of attention that the person can give to outside matters, such as work or other people. They can completely withdraw from interacting with other people, because it's almost more than they can manage to cope with what's going on inside their self.

More profoundly, there are many ways by which people have developed low confidence and low self-esteem and thus feel insecure. And if someone has suffered from one of these, you might well find that they have suffered from a whole lot of them. Here are some of the more common ones:

- Taking negatives literally and personally when someone says something like 'you are stupid' or 'you'll never amount to anything' (often described as 'taking things to heart' or 'taking things personally').
- Confusing 'having been no good at *doing* something' (ie past tense, behavioural, and easy to change through learning and practising new behaviours) with 'being' no good (ie never-ending present/future tense, right at the heart of one's identity).
- Comparing themselves to someone who's really good at something after years of practice, whereas they're just beginning.
- Predicting the future from past events that have gone wrong, eg 'I'm bound to get the blame, as usual' or 'She'll again just tell me it's rubbish.'

Many people can pin down their lack of confidence, and their feelings of insecurity, to a specific event, or to one person's influence. For example, if they have received enough 'You are stupid' statements (present tense, global), then the impact of those statements can perniciously switch into an internalized belief that colours how they see *everything* (eg 'I am stupid').

Tips for handling insecure people

There are many ways of helping, by giving them space, supportively and sensitively.

Be specific

If in doubt, be specific. Help them to think and talk about specifics. For example, if someone says something like 'I am hopeless at X', get down to details with, say, 'What exactly have you found difficult about X? What could make it easier in future?' This shifts from

- the personal
- the present tense
- a blanket 'truth'

to helping the person to start thinking about

- the behavioural
- the past and future, separately
- specifics.

This approach helps them to separate their past failures from future events, and might initially cause stunned confusion in the person, especially if they have become accustomed to feeling hopeless just by saying, 'I am hopeless...'

But remember that your response clearly separates a 'past' that felt hopeless, a present where you are both talking about specifics, and a future that *could* feel easier. The other person may have been (past tense!) unlikely to have ever thought about such events specifically, rather than in a panicky confusion.

Three other factors are worth noting here:

- First, the use of the word 'exactly' helps people to know that they are to focus on detail rather than get lost in the confusion of their thoughts.

■ Second, you are respecting their position, not denying it (as in 'Of course you're not hopeless at X.').

■ Third, by asking the question 'What exactly have you found difficult about it?' and staying with them, you are helping them simply by being there, supportively, rather than leaving them alone to – possibly – slip back into an even worse state (eg 'Not only am I hopeless at X, I can't even explain why!').

Not just blanket but universal

The statement in the previous tip – 'I am hopeless at X' – at least is confined to X. Compare this with a universal statement such as 'I am pathetic/stupid/hopeless/no good.'

A useful response, and one that takes them literally, is to ask, for example, 'At all things?' This respects their statement rather than denying it (eg 'Of course you're not!'), while challenging them to think *about* what they have said, rather than to act it out, again. It also depersonalizes it to a behavioural level ('things' rather than 'I am...')

You might also try changing the context of their statement from a universal one to a specific one. So, you might ask them about home – for example: 'So, how are you at sport, cooking, driving? What do you enjoy doing?' And when you get a little bite (eg 'Well, I suppose people do enjoy my cooking...'), you can draw them out by, first, getting them to talk more about what they clearly *can* do – and ensure that you help them to realize that they've been doing that for a long time, building up their abilities and confidence step by step, skill by skill, compared to all the new things they are finding at work.

You could then ask them what else they enjoy (ie are good at) doing and then point out to them, gently of course, that their opening statement 'I'm pathetic/stupid/hopeless/no good' could not have been strictly true!

Finally, and usefully, move forward gently by asking, for example, 'So what help do you need, exactly, to build your... skills, just as you've built your cooking skills?' And be prepared for this to take time while they think about hitherto unthought-of possibilities.

Keep it behavioural

Stick to what the person did or said (behaviourally) and avoid totally who they 'are' (identity). This is an essential rule of feedback in any case, so that people can identify precisely what they did well, and therefore know what to continue doing. For example:

- ■ 'Your presentation was clear and to the point' (not 'You are a good presenter').
- ■ 'You give the trainees confidence by working alongside them to answer their questions as they arise' (not 'You are good with trainees').

Boundaries

In all cases, remember who you are: possibly their boss, or colleague or friend, and probably not their full-time fully supervised trained counsellor or therapist. However well meaning you are, you have your own job to do, and life to live, and cannot be on call for them all the time.

Out of your depth

Be aware also that there are some people whose sense of insecurity is so rock-bottom that *almost nothing* you try will work. In these cases, you might even suspect some form of clinical depression, so don't meddle! The best help you can give is to consult with an expert and – here's the exception to the 'almost nothing' above – to support the person while they get the appropriate professional help.

Stick to work

There is often such a lot going on 'inside' the person that any external interference, however well intentioned, can cause whatever is going on to fall apart, spill out or even explode. Unless it's relevant to their performance at work, it's not normally appropriate or desirable to pry or interfere.

Stay on the surface

The safest way to avoid getting into deep water is to keep conversations about work at an impersonal behavioural level – for example: 'Will there be a problem with that deadline?' rather than 'Will you be having a problem with that deadline?'

And if you've noticed that they are avoiding conversations about non-work subjects – eg family, weekends, friends – keep conversations to work topics that are relevant to you both.

Follow their lead

Since there's such a lot going on inside, just smile and leave them alone. This is a clear friendly message that you're not crowding them, or prying.

'Not even little ripples, please'

I remember someone coming to the third session of a training course I was running, having missed the first two with no advance warning. Immediately they arrived, they explained that they might have to leave early, and then went to sit alone, clutching the back of their chair, which they had moved to an empty space near the door.

At the first break they rushed up to me, explained that they knew all this stuff anyway, and rushed out. I later heard that they'd been coping with illness, divorce and more, and – quite rightly – didn't feel able to cope with any more.

I remembered how they'd been clutching onto their chair like a life raft, and the expression 'keeping your head above water' came to mind. I can understand that if someone is just about managing to 'keep their head above water', the last thing they need is someone making waves, or even ripples.

'JFK'

When people think they 'should' know everything, I often remind them of this story.

President John F Kennedy was, it is said, very confident when speaking with small groups of people, but felt very insecure when speaking to large groups. His coach, Dorothy Sarner, encouraged him to think of several things to give him confidence. Three of them are particularly worth passing on to someone who is about to give a talk or presentation. Just think:

- ■ 'I'm glad you're here' – because, without this thought, we might be scowling anxiously or staring at the carpet as we think, for example, 'I'm really nervous in front of you lot!'
- ■ 'I'm glad *I'm* here.'
- ■ 'I know what I know' – that is to say, I have all the information with me that I have with me, and no more than that, but no *less* than that, either. I can answer what I can answer. So I can also know when to respond, say, 'I need to get back to you on that. Let's talk later.' Or 'I haven't been briefed on that yet.' Or 'I don't know, Mike. You tell me!'

'And finally...'

Some people feel 'under pressure' or 'stressed out' as they 'strive to be perfect' or are always 'running to keep ahead of themselves'. They might find this story useful.

Carl Rogers, a well-known psychotherapist, was asked how he was so successful at what he did. He replied 'Before a session with a client I remind myself that I Am Enough. I am not "perfect" and, in any case, "perfect" is not human, and would not be enough. But I am human, and there is nothing that this client can say or do or feel that I cannot feel in myself. So I can be with them. I am enough.'

25

Insincere people

*who may also be seen as Deceivers, Liars,
Manipulators, Tricksters, Two-faced, Untrustworthy*

What ticks us off

When someone says one thing and does another, we can feel
deceived or tricked or manipulated.

How it can happen

We're not talking about little 'white lies' here. For example, if
you're asked by someone who's about to go to a wedding
whether you like their hat, the consequences of saying that it's
grotesque are unthinkable, compared to a sweet 'Fine.' (And, in
any case, we wouldn't have been asked if the person didn't
know the truth. We're being invited into their game of 'let's
pretend', so that they don't feel so alone with the truth! They
know you hesitated just a smidgeon before you answered, and
will always love you for being true to yourself, and kind to
them.)

We *are* talking about contradictory or mixed messages. If
someone says 'with all due respect' and then says something
disrespectful, we are clearly being led to believe one thing, and
then later find out that something was hidden from us. For
example:

- The person says one thing and subsequently does another.
- A promise is made and not kept.
- Someone says 'no', but looks interested (and then may take the idea as their own).

When we eventually realize that we have been fooled (eg by feeling foolish or angry, or understanding that we have been manipulated or tricked or undermined), it often happens that we say something like 'Do you know, I had a funny feeling at the time...' or 'I knew something like this would happen.' Somehow, we picked up on what we heard from the other person, but didn't act on what we ourselves felt.

Tips for handling insincere people

Respect your gut feel

If you have a 'funny feeling', then respect that, and take a little time to ask yourself what exactly you are feeling uncertain (or scared or unsettled or whatever) about. If necessary, refuse to be hurried into a decision and say you need a little time to think about it. (I often say something like 'That sounds really good/interesting/appealing to me, and so I'd like some time to consider what I *feel* about it.')

Confront gently but firmly

Once you have identified the mixed messages (and there are often just two), ask the person which of them you should act upon – for example: 'You said that this was a great idea I had, but you've not done anything with it, so what is your true position, please?' or 'I know you said that "with respect" it would be good for my career to do exactly as you tell me to do, but I remember that the last time I did that, you took the credit, so what are you planning to do this time, please?'

Confront, then assert

Rather than asking for clarification on mixed messages, you could explain that you noticed both messages, and then introduce a third element that feels right for you and puts the action back where it belongs – under your control. For example: 'You said that this was a great idea I had, but you've not done anything with it, so I've progressed it myself, thanks.' Or 'I know you said that "with respect" it would be good for my career to do exactly as you tell me to do, but I remember the last time I did that, you took the credit and I got overlooked, so this time I'd feel safer doing what I feel I should do, and start looking after my own career, thanks.'

Keep it behavioural

Avoid branding someone's entire identity (ie the 'you' in the following examples), eg 'You are a liar' or 'You deceive people' or 'I could never trust you again.'

Ensure that you keep the conversation flowing about what exactly was or wasn't *said* or *done* – for example: 'You agreed that I should do X and then wrote a memo against it. Help me to understand the situation please, as I'm confused right now.'

Calling someone a 'liar', say, can provoke profound, long-lasting hostility, as it rejects their entire identity (ie 'them') in a one-dimensional, dismissive and negative way. And no one likes to be summed up like that.

26

Last-minuters

who leave things until the very last moment

What ticks us off

It can be stressful if almost everyone in a team prepares well ahead of time, but one or more people leave things as late as they can. However much they may explain that that's how they prefer to work, it can be a nail-biting time for other team members.

How it can happen

Some people like the increasing sense of energy and excitement as they work closer and closer to a deadline. Others physically need the pressure of a looming deadline. And maybe there's also a pattern of not believing deadlines that have been set, and smelling a 'false deadline' for what it is. In all these cases there's also a valid justification in allowing the maximum 'thinking' time before the 'doing' time.

On another track, some people may actually need help in planning their time.

Tips for handling last-minuters

Openness – 1

Openness is the only policy that's likely to be effective. Be open about how you feel – for example:

- ■ 'I need the whole team to have a full run-through at X pm on Y day.'
- ■ 'For my own reassurance, I need to see what you propose at A pm on B day in its finished form.'

Openness – 2

Stay open-minded, and if the person who has been causing anxiety has shown that they do in fact deliver on time, remember that *how* people do what they do is very individual, and it may cramp someone's style to insist on a different approach from them. However, if it's a consistent problem, you have every right to discuss it with them and to work out other ways for 1) them to work, and 2) you to feel reassured.

In very extreme cases, however, your expectations and their preferences might be mutually incompatible and you may need some help to be flexible. (Otherwise you could only work with people who are 'like you', and that limits everyone's field, doesn't it?)

Meeting expectations

If people have been unaware of how other people plan their time, it may be useful to help them with a simple model. I like this one, as it breaks a task into separate stages and assumes that they will be spread over time, not done in one big 'go'. The key is to allocate a length of time for each stage, to get a feel for not only how long it'll take, but also how exactly you plan to do it. Here's an example for a successful presentation and, yes, it is spelled out step by step because missing out any stage can easily lead to missing the goal:

1. Discuss what exactly is needed with each potential attendee:
   a. 10 minutes writing e-mail request;
   b. 10 minutes × 6 people follow-up phone calls.
2. Define purpose of presentation:
   a. 10 minutes thinking;
   b. 10 minutes drafting;
   c. 5 minutes × 3 people checking it out by phone;
   d. 20 minutes finalizing;
   e. 2 minutes sending out confirmatory e-mail.
3. Write presentation:
   a. 20 minutes thinking;
   b. 20 minutes drafting outline;
   c. 5 minutes × 3 people checking it out by phone;
   d. 20 minutes writing draft 2;
   e. 20 minutes revising final draft.
4. Presentation:
   a. 5 minutes reminding attendees of agreed purpose from 1b) and 2e);
   b. 1 minute headline;
   c. 15 minutes justification of headline, with questions;
   d. Repeat of 1 minute headline and 15 minutes justification of headline, with questions, for each section;
   e. 5 minutes summary of next steps, and agree draft minutes.
5. Post-presentation:
   a. 5 minutes × 6 people following up on next steps and their satisfaction with meeting, to avoid unresolved issues remaining hidden;
   b. 15 minutes writing the minutes.

(This has been a complete revelation, simple though it might seem, to some people who have been used to 'writing a presentation' an hour before it's due. And, to be fair, if they've never thought of all the stages that might be needed, they've been doing pretty well up to now, luckily.)

27

Late people

who may also consistently Miss Deadlines or be
Unpunctual or Unreliable

What ticks us off

We all know the person who consistently arrives late, misses deadlines and gets all flustered in the process. Or, astonishingly, they seem completely unflustered and truly surprised that this has happened, again.

Please note, by 'late people' I'm not referring to dead people, although the terms 'dead-lines' and 'you're dead if you're late again' spring to mind!

How it can happen

A very common reason for being late, is – strangely – to have the time they should arrive, or should deliver the report, very clearly in mind. That's why they get taken aback: 'But I knew the time I was aiming for.' And that's the problem. The time they have in mind is the time of arrival, not the time they need to leave in order to arrive on time. Or they are fixed on the time to deliver the package and haven't factored backwards, with the time to physically take it there, pack it up and get it together in the first place. So, when the arrival time arrives, it's a real surprise that they can't get there on time!

Tips for handling late people

Work backwards

When they've missed a deadline, ask them 'how exactly' they missed it, step by step, so that you can help them to find a better way (and it might be better if you did this at a relaxed time rather than in the heat of the moment). You could also ask them to reassure you by detailing exactly how – step by step again – they will get an item to you by the agreed deadline next time.

Maybe suggest they work backwards – for instance:

■ I need to arrive at 6.00.
■ 10-minute walk from car park (so leave car at 5.50).
■ 10 minutes to find parking space at that time of day (so arrive in area at 5.40).
■ 30 minutes to drive at that time of day (so drive off at 5.10).
■ 10 minutes to get to car (so leave at 5.00).
■ 15 minutes to pack, and remember to make forgotten phone call.
■ So, 4.45 is the Start to Leave Time to remember.

'A real dead line'

I was staying in a hostel, many years ago, and at 10 pm one evening the fire bell went off. We all came to the assembly point, checked the signing-in book and found that (let's call her) Laura wasn't present. After much discussion (Was it a real fire? Was it just a practice? Would it be safe to go and look for Laura?), she joined us at about 10.20 looking very flustered and upset. 'I'm sorry I'm late, but I was so tired that I went straight to bed without putting my clothes out for the next day. Now I always plan what I'm going to wear and get my clothes ready the night before, so I can dress and leave on time in the morning, but because I didn't do it tonight, when the bell went off I just couldn't decide what to wear!'

28

Loners

*who may also Keep Themselves to Themselves and
not be Obvious Team Players*

What ticks us off

Loners don't join in. It's an effort to get them involved. And
this may be true on both the work and the social fronts.

How it can happen

Often these people just quietly get on with their job and are
simply more intravert (meaning turning inwards) than
extravert (turning outwards). Perhaps they are the slow, steady
type who prefer to follow their own train of thought rather
than have it interrupted by other people? Maybe they have
more than enough team playing at home, and are happier to be
left alone so long as they do their job satisfactorily. It could also
be that they are better at observing and thinking before talking.
Any one of these patterns can single someone out as a loner,
whereas in reality there's absolutely nothing wrong with their
performance.

Tips for handling loners

Great expectations

If we are expecting everyone to be the life and soul of the party, we are probably excluding over 80 per cent of the population. Certainly some jobs need a high level of team participation (eg party entertainers), but many do not. Check out the job's *person* specification (not skills or tasks specification) to ensure that the required level of camaraderie is clearly specified.

Remember also that many 'fun' people are spending more time having 'fun' than the steady loner who can always be relied upon to do what's required without a fuss.

Is it really so important that they come for a drink with everyone, even if they feel uncomfortable?

Look. Ask!

Some people are uncomfortable around 'loners' because they themselves feel rejected or uninvolved. They want to 'cheer them up' or 'get them involved'.

1. Have a good look at your own motivations.
2. Then have a good look at the person concerned. Do they seem to have a problem?
   - If yes, maybe gently ask 'OK?', which at least will register your concern without expecting a long response.
   - If they seem content, maybe gently say 'Hello', and then stop fretting!

Notice that each of the above ('OK' and 'Hello') is just one word, which is probably much more on their wavelength than volumes and volumes, yes?

Come straight out with it

Another approach that is often greatly appreciated in a very quiet way is to mention to the person in a quiet moment that you've noticed that they are at the quieter end of the spectrum compared with some of their colleagues.

Reassure them that there's absolutely nothing wrong with that. And then ask if everything's OK, or if there's any problem, or if – wait for it – they are just at the quieter end of the spectrum, and quite content, thank you! Very often you might have been worrying unnecessarily, or filling in the gaps when there really weren't any to fill in.

Cut the cloth

Loners may often be less assertive than other team members unless they are 'pushed too far' or feel too uncomfortable. So, be aware that trying to bring them out of themselves and into the team could be unnecessarily hard work for you and for them.

They might actually prefer to be behind the pillar, or in the corner, and thereby feel less pressure to get involved and to be jolly at all times. Check it out with them. Ask.

29

Messy people

who may also be Disorganized or Untidy

What ticks us off

'A messy desk shows a messy mind', it is said. An untidy room (especially a child's bedroom) seems to be the eighth deadly sin. We seem to associate disorder with discomfort, and then need to re-establish order: for example, that picture isn't quite straight, that bed isn't turned down properly. And, irritatingly, it may not seem to bother the 'messy' person one little bit.

How it can happen

There are several patterns that can overlap.

Inconsistency

If we haven't allocated precise and consistent places for putting things (eg a filing system, or 'in', 'out' and 'pending' trays, or a key hook by the front door), then we put our files or keys… well, wherever we put them at the time, making it harder to locate them later, because of the inconsistency with which we placed them in the first place.

Horizontal filing

Some people believe that having piles of things 'all over the place' is effective for them, and that they know exactly where to find things. But this can bother other people hugely, as it seems that the person's piles are going to spread and invade other people's territory and – quite rightly – that if the person is away, it'll be very time-consuming to find anything.

Not very visual

Some people simply are not very visual and just don't notice or register the mess, or the crooked picture on the wall. They can be quite surprised if these are pointed out to them, as they quite simply hadn't seen them, let alone 'seen' them as a 'problem'.

Not minding

And there are people who can see the visual 'clutter' but are not affected by it, or don't mind it – it's not a problem because it's not important to them. (This is *inexplicable* to people who 'need' to have things ordered and orderly!)

 ✓ TIP

Tips for handling messy people

Apart from matters of security, is a 'clean desk' policy the best one for everyone? To judge by the patterns outlined above, not necessarily! So, maybe we can accept that so long as 'their' mess doesn't impinge on anyone else, that's their problem – or not!

That's a bit harder to accept where there is 'shared territory' such as a refreshment room or open-plan offices or hot-desking, but the strategy that follows has tended to work well, no matter what the causal pattern has been.

Ground rules

Sit down at a calm-ish time (ie not when there's a specific untidiness issue) and discuss what matters to each of you, and separate it into:

■ what is essential for you personally; and
■ what would be nice but is not essential.

Cover the essentials first. No one should need to compromise on what – to them – is essential. Then agree on what you all *want* (but leave the *how* until later).

And then get the 'offenders' to suggest what penalties would be appropriate if they don't fulfil their agreed obligations. (And maybe agree what rewards might be appropriate – but beware of rewarding 'normal' behaviour with more than a 'thank you', otherwise you may become trapped into having to reward them constantly.)

Then get all this written down – the *whats* and the accompanying rewards and penalties. Notice that this is still only *what* you have all agreed, and you've not yet covered *how* or *when*. (This is important, as many plans get confused by bringing in the *how* too soon.)

Then ask each person how and when they might fulfil their obligations. Encourage them to think creatively, because they've not been brilliant at this in the past, have they, otherwise it would not still be a subject for discussion! And make sure that they have a range of several *how* and *when* options to choose from. And leave the choice to them. Remember, the important commitment is to *what* will happen, not *how*.

Reward compliance and enforce the penalties, no matter what excuses there are! The penalties were suggested by the 'offender', and you may want to remind them of this, pointing to what was written down at the time. After all, if you don't enforce the penalty, then it undermines the fact that this was 'essential' to someone.

'What??!!'

A friend was fed up with her children leaving their toys, clothes, rubbish, etc all over the house. We discussed the above strategy, and she had a successful chat with all concerned, drawing up the ground rules and penalties, and getting everyone to sign and date it (a nice added touch).

I later got an astonished call to say that it had worked. The children had agreed that anything that was not in its place would be regarded as rubbish, and Mum would therefore put it out with the rubbish.

That morning, when the children couldn't find their school uniforms and school bags that they'd left lying around, Mum calmly told them that she'd put them out with the rubbish, as agreed. They were horrified! They rushed outside, only to find that this was true, and hurriedly got dressed in somewhat crumpled clothes. But this never needed to happen again. Mum simply had to remind them of the consequences, and of 'rubbish day'.

She also had added some rather elegant and imaginative touches. She knew that there was no rubbish collection that day. She knew that the children liked to look smart and not crumpled. She also knew that they would think that she had put their things in with empty food cans and other messy items, whereas she had (sensibly) chosen to put them in a separate new rubbish bag. And she took time later to ensure that they had enough hangers and hooks for 'tidying away' the offending items in the first place.

They laugh about it now, but she still reminds them that she has the signed ground rules!

30

Moody people

who may also seem Temperamental, Unpredictable and/or Unreliable

What ticks us off

We might be very cautious around moody or temperamental people because, from our past experiences of them, we don't know how they are going to react. It cramps our style, and concerns us that we might have a 'loose cannon' in our midst, one that might 'go off' at any time. It's unsettling.

How it can happen

The person concerned might be clinically, physically or emotionally depressed, or have a 'bipolar' disorder (which used to be called 'manic depression', as the person's moods can swing dramatically and unpredictably). Alternatively, they might have a huge amount to cope with, inside and/or outside work, and be somewhat overloaded and preoccupied.

In either case, it's very hard for them to cope, not surprisingly, and sometimes the internal partitions that hold things in place might burst – and whoever happens to be around at the time gets the full force of the spillage.

Tips for handling moody people

Be sensitive

Whatever their mood, respect it. If they are quiet and 'down', don't try to cheer them 'up' as it could overload their 'I'm Trying My Best to Keep It All Together' efforts.

Be there

A quiet 'OK' or 'Hello' can speak volumes compared to speaking volumes! (Many people who have been very depressed have reported how a quiet word touched them very deeply, because it made no demands on them.)

Be honest

If you happened to be around when there was an outburst, check it out – for example: 'Mike, was it something I did or said, or did I just happen to be there at the time?' (Calling a person by name – first name or Mr/Ms/Mrs X, whatever is usual – helps to touch a person quite deeply.)

If it *was* something you said or did, good! Now it's in the open, you can apologize because you didn't mean them to be upset, and fix a time to talk things through.

If it was nothing to do with you – you just happened to be there – the other person is probably upset that they upset you, and again it gets this into the open and gives you a chance to chat.

Be useful

Whatever the events may be, let the person know that you're happy to help, if you can. You might want to leave the ball in their court, to avoid pressuring them. Or you might want to arrange periodic meetings, drinks, etc where they can voice any concerns – but where that is not the prime purpose of meeting. In any case, be aware that if someone is very 'down', they rarely have the energy to face bringing things up.

Be realistic

Unless you are a doctor, therapist, psychiatrist, psychologist or counsellor, remember that you are not a doctor, therapist, psychiatrist, psychologist or counsellor! Don't get out of your depth, and encourage the person to consult with professionals if you feel that is appropriate. And yes, this could seem as though you're giving them the brush-off, but not if you offer to take them or accompany them if they'd like that.

31

Must-have-the-last-word people

who may also be Hangers-on and The Last To Leave

What ticks us off

They just have to have the last word on everything. The chair of the meeting may have summed up 'So we've agreed X, Y and Z. Thanks everyone.' And our friend pipes up 'And W?' or 'I agree' or whatever they might say. It doesn't really matter. They just have to have the last word. Don't they? Yes. They do. And so on. And on. And on.

How it can happen

With some people there's an insecurity as if they need to be noticed by other people or even, maybe, by themselves. With others there's a triumphal arrogance or smugness, as if their voice is the only one truly worth hearing, and by having the *last* word they have somehow 'won' the situation or argument or even conversation.

We can speculate about the causes of these but, whatever the causes, the pattern shows simply that they do not know how to exit comfortably. Whether it's a conversation, a room, a meeting, a meal, a holiday – you get the picture – their exits are uncomfortable. For us, and for them.

Tips for handling Must-Have-The-Last-Worders

Be upfront

Let's be honest, this is a behavioural trait that should have been covered in their regular one-to-one meetings with their manager, and/or set as a target in their personal development plan, and/or written into their appraisal. We're not saying that they are a bad person – far from it – so let's reframe their behaviour here, eg 'your desire to contribute while meetings are wrapping up or closing down is enthusiastic but inappropriate, and I'd like you to develop other ways of contributing in a timely way, and leaving meetings and conversations content-edly, instead of obviously trying to ensure that the last word is yours'. And have three examples ready. And then change the subject to avoid it hanging like blame in the air. It's just some new behaviours that we want them to add to their repertoire, so that they can exit comfortably.

Show them the exit

Many people don't know how to exit even a conversation let alone a meeting, so, for example, if they are paid a compliment, eg 'what a great tie!', they mutter ashamedly that it was in a sale, and had a loose thread and so on and so on. Instead of just saying 'Thank You!' and then changing the subject, to avoid that ghastly pregnant pause hanging in midair. There's nothing else to be said. You complimented me. I thanked you. Job done. Short sentences. Move on.

So maybe we can tell them about this Tie Compliment Syndrome and how, when someone pays a compliment all that's needed is a 'Thank You!' and a change of subject. And we could point out that 'Thank You!' or 'Thanks Everyone!' is a great exit line from *any* type of situation, followed by turning on our heels and exiting. Or we could suggest putting down the phone with a clear 'Goodbye!' or 'See you soon/next time!' Short, clear sentences followed by an exit.

Rituals

I must be frank here: it took me a long time to realize that when someone asks 'How are you?' they're generally not enquiring about my health. And when I'm asked 'How (are) you doing?' I really don't need to go through my balance sheet with them. These are ritual greetings (ie *entry* lines) that generally require simply (1) a polite 'Fine, thank you' (or similar) followed by (2) a simple and not over-solicitous 'And you?'

In e-mails and letters they may be statements rather than questions, eg 'I hope you're well' and, because they're not questions, they don't need answers. (Naturally we're not talking here about conversations over a drink or a meal or a weekend, where the whole point is to 'catch up' with how 'things' are.)

And – while I'm in confessional mode – I confess that it took me some time to realize that 'See you soon/next time!' doesn't need me to take this literally and get out my diary and ask 'When?' Nor does 'We must have lunch sometime...' or 'Let's do this again soon...'. I eventually learnt that '... sometime...' and '... soon...' are just exit rituals that have no meaning in themselves, other than cordiality!

OK, just push them through the exit!

Despite all our best efforts, there may still be a few remaining Hangers-On. It may be perfectly obvious to us that the conversation or meeting is over, whether face to face or on the phone. We've run out of small talk and even very small talk. We've pointedly said 'Thanks. It was great talking with you on this. See you soon. Goodbye.' but they're still there, hanging around. They *still* don't seem to have got the message.

We must be then be absolutely upfront, while keeping the tone of voice friendly but firm. 'I think that's it for this conversation, yes? Anything else at your end, Pat? Right. We're done then. Thanks Pat/everybody.' and immediately leave, or hang up the phone. And, vitally, we must remember our exit routine and use the same words and tone of voice as a ritual in the future.

They'll eventually get the message and if they don't we can tell them, eg 'Pat, when I say "Right. We're done then. Thanks Pat/everybody." we can all go. That's the clear sign that we're finished. OK?' And then we change the subject, as a clear sign that we've exited from this topic!

32

Negative people

*who may also be But-ters, Dampeners, Pessimists
or Wet Blankets*

What ticks us off

It gets really demoralizing when we have this great idea and
someone pours a bucket of cold water all over it (and us) time
after time. All with the words 'Yes, but...'

In fact, it gets so that we don't want these people around us.
We don't invite them to meetings. We don't seek out their opinions. Because they're such downers!

How it can happen

The cause is very simple.

First, when the word 'but' is used, it acts like an erase button, making us forget everything that came before. So we
remember the problems after the 'but' rather than the 'yes'
points before it.

Second, it takes many more words to explain what's wrong
with something than to explain what's right – so the impression
can be that there's a lot wrong and not a lot that's right. See for
yourself by describing a 'bad' cup of tea (eg too strong, weak,
hot, cold, milky, bitter, big, small) and a 'good' cup (eg just
right, nice, um, er).

Third, and critically, 'negative' people naturally see what could go *wrong* rather than what could go *right*. Not deliberately, but naturally. That's what their brain presents them with first. That's how they're wired.

Tips for handling negative people

Be grateful

Look on them in a new light. Welcome and encourage their comments, knowing that their insights could save you and your organization a lot of expensive mistakes because they are more aware of the potentially problematic details in a situation, whereas you yourself might have only seen the positive big picture.

Don't take it personally

They are seeing things that could genuinely enhance parts of your plan if they are given attention. Grit your teeth and ask, 'So what other pitfalls might stop this working?' or 'What other potential problems occur to you?'

Be realistic

Don't expect the same level of enthusiasm from them as you yourself have for the idea. They're seeing the potential problems and are unlikely to get excited by them. (The best you can hope for is a 'Not really' when you ask 'So, if we pay attention to all these things, is there any other reason why this might not succeed?')

33

Nit-picky people

who may tend to Find Faults

What ticks us off

How irritating it is when people have a tendency to pick holes in other people's ideas, in what they say, in what they wear, in – well, everything, it seems.

How it can happen

We're not talking here about people who are deliberately doing this as part of a get-my-own-back revenge campaign, or a grudge. We're talking about almost involuntary behaviours:

- First, some people tend to focus on what's wrong, rather than what's right.
- Second, while other people may tend to see the 'big picture', some nit-picky people are much more attracted by detail.
- And third, in some people these two patterns combine and can give their body almost a physical jolt when something 'stands out like a sore thumb' – it's as if they are physically incapable of noticing the other, healthy thumb and fingers at all!

And so – whichever of these patterns is operating – their mouth opens and the nit-picking begins, often point by point instead of waiting until the end of the sentence or presentation or whatever.

Tips for handling nit-picky people

There's little point in trying to stop them – that will have been tried many times before, and it's still not broken the pattern.

A quiet word

It's unlikely that they are unaware of this pattern of behaviour, and it's probable that they 'can't help themselves'. So, you have to help them. Find a time when you can both talk 'about' this pattern, rather than when you are both 'in' it. And since you need to recognize that you won't be able to stop the tendency they have, here are some practical ideas for managing how they act on it:

- 'I want you to put a finger on your lips, not from your writing hand, to keep your lips together (as works well for little children in schools, for a short while); the rest of us will just see you looking thoughtful.'
- 'I want you to write down all the points you want to make, as we do want to hear them, but only after you've heard everything that's being said, not interruption by interruption.'
- 'Please then look at everything you've written and see if you can categorize some of it into clusters, or "big-picture" thoughts, for us.'
- 'And all of this is because we value what you input, but there are ways in which you can make it easier for us to accept how you do it.'

The art of being wise

The art of being wise includes the skill of knowing what to overlook, and it might be interesting to explore this with the nit-picking person, again in a quiet moment. Some people have a feeling that they are the world's policeman or policewoman, and it is their *duty* to pick up on other people's mistakes, errors, omissions, grammatical errors, misspellings – and it's so *tiring* for them to be on duty all the time.

Whatever their reasons for doing this, and they can be many and varied, you can reassure them that you're happy to let little details slide, so long as they are not vital. For example, if everyone knows that someone meant Janice but said Janet, it doesn't need to be pointed out immediately and in public, perhaps?

It can be very powerful for someone to be given this permission to overlook every little detail, especially as you can reassure them that their brain is blessed with an ability to notice these things, but you are relieving them of the 'duty', at work at least, to point out every single one.

34

Patronizing people

who may also be Arrogant, Belittling, Insensitive, Pompous, Self-important, Smug, Snobbish, Thick-skinned, Unobservant or all of these at once

What ticks us off

Quite simply, no one likes to feel belittled, treated like dirt, ignored, diminished or dismissed – that is, to feel small. (Indeed, making people feel this way is a form of bullying.)

How it can happen

For whatever reason, people who make us feel belittled think they are 'better' people than the rest of us. Maybe they were told so as a child – for example: 'You're my best boy' or 'You're the cleverest girl I know.'

Or maybe they think they are *less* 'good' and are putting on an act, to cover up how they really feel.

In either case, they – consciously or unwittingly – try to demonstrate this in what they do or say, or how they do or say it.

Tips for handling patronizing people

Self-protection

We must not take this personally! Whatever their opinion is of who we are, we need to remember that they are only acting pompously (or patronizingly or whatever it seems like) by voicing an *opinion* (of theirs) and pretending that it's a *fact*.

We need also to remember that it is based on something we did or said, not – as they are presenting it – as a final view on who we are as a person!

It's also possible that if the person acts that way in general, it's not aimed at us specifically.

And in any case, we are able to look beyond how someone presents themself, to what they are actually communicating.

Showing respect – 1 (showing but not necessarily feeling it!)

This could be called flattery, but let's just call it respect here, because it's a practical two-step way of moving forward:

1. Show respect for their self-image (knowing it's only a self-image); then,
2. Get to the point.

For example, you might say 'I know you're very busy with a lot of high-level issues right now, but I need three detailed minutes with you so I can get a very clear brief of what exactly you need from me, please.'

Showing respect – 2 (in a twisted sort of way)

Another way of addressing this, and getting the person to laugh along with you – even if they are not sure why – is to pretend that they must have been joking and that you had fallen for their joke. For example, you could say (with a smile on your face and a twinkle in your eyes) 'Do you know, you were sounding so patronizing then that for one moment I thought you were being serious!' And then – with no more than a small pause – say something else to move the situation on, such as 'So what exactly you were suggesting is X? Can you tell me some more about that, please?'

Skills or self?

Some people have a keen sense of people's positions and equate a 'high' organizational position with a high value as a person. I know people who talk of managers as 'high-ups' or 'superiors'. This is a throwback to Victorian snobbery at its worst! A 'higher' position should reflect a higher level of valued skills, not a reflection on the person's value as a human being. (Personally, I believe that all people have absolutely identical worth as people, but absolutely varied levels of skills and preferences – and that these should not be confused!) Moreover, having a mindset with 'high-ups', 'superiors' or 'uppers' can lead one to label others as 'low-downs', 'inferiors' or 'subordinates'. This might be useful to the snob, but is not conducive to healthy team working.

So let's refer to people simply by their job titles (eg directors, managers, level threes).

Criterial equivalents (what?!)

We might have met someone who had a specific way of talking and who 'made us feel small', and since then we've had a tendency to 'feel small' whenever we've heard that way of talking. (And we might not have noticed when people who had that way of talking *didn't* 'make us feel small'!)

Or we might have had great colleagues from a specific country in the past and we have subsequently had a predisposition to like other people from that country. (And to feel let down by them if 'they' didn't live up to our expectations!)

In these examples, the 'criteria' for judging were the way of talking and the country of origin, and we had latched onto them – unwittingly perhaps – as evidence of a whole set of expectations from everyone with these criteria. (Other examples are people who – from experiences with one particular person – generalize and think, say, that blue eyes promise kindness, or that tall people are strong.)

A simple way of getting past this is:

- to recognize our foibles in this respect (eg liking (all) Australians; being nervous about (all) posh-sounding people); and then
- to focus on *what* exactly they are saying or doing, rather than on how they have been doing it.

'Smile'

I remember seeing the tall, posh-sounding comedian Stephen Fry standing up and talking down to the less tall, less posh-sounding journalist Ian Hislop. Ian stood up at one point, with a twinkle in his eye and a smile on his face, and shook Stephen's hand, saying 'It's such a privilege to be patronized by you, Stephen!'

Name-droppers

Some people assume that by dropping names of famous people they are putting themselves on the same 'level' as them. This is quite easy to deal with, again by, first, respecting their ploy, and then focusing on the matter in hand – for example: 'I understand that you've been saying that Winston Churchill and John F Kennedy always did X, but right now I want to know what exactly *you* are proposing in our *particular* situation?' And, as usual, be prepared to invite the person to go away and think about it.

Phobic people

*who may be Fearful, Frightened, Scared or
Terrified of, say, presenting in public*

What ticks us off

Some people are disabled by fears that prevent them from performing 'normally' at work. They might even have a massive reaction to the very thought of whatever they are phobic to. It might be spiders or snakes or – in the workplace – confined spaces, flying or, very commonly, presenting. (It is said that the human brain is a fantastic instrument: it starts working long before birth; it carries on developing throughout life; and then it suddenly stops functioning when its owner is standing up in front of an audience!)

Even at the very thought of their phobia, the person goes hot and sweaty, or cold and clammy, or whatever their particular way of 'doing' phobias might be.

How it can happen

Richard Bandler and John Grinder described a common type of phobia as where the person's response is significantly greater than whatever stimulated that response. For example, actually being attacked by a snake or assaulted by an audience at a presentation would naturally provoke a strong reaction, but this would be appropriate to the event, and therefore not a phobia. However, if the person has a similar severe reaction when just *thinking* of a snake or presentation, or just by seeing or hearing the word 'snake' or 'presentation', then that is what is defined here as a phobia.

Bandler and Grinder understood that, with a phobia, the body is simply reacting to a thought that is in turn based on a memory of a pretty traumatic event. (That event might have been real or it might have been vividly imagined: some people have developed phobias after hearing a story or having a dream.)

Importantly, they realized that the traumatic event – real or imagined – shocked the body into producing maximum adrenaline to kick us into 'fight or flight' mode, and that that swamp-load of adrenaline drowned out one other very important memory: that the person survived the event. And that's why the stimulus – even just the name on a piece of paper – can produce the same 'I'm going to die/suffocate/be killed' response.

Subsequent research into post-traumatic stress syndrome has validated their work and, moreover, found that the swamp-load of adrenaline completely overloads the short-term memory store, and instead of the event merely being processed into long-term memory as a conceptual memory, the adrenaline production shoots straight into long-term memory too and is locked together with the conceptual memory of the event. Hence, seeing the word can trigger not only the memory, but also the added adrenaline.

So, back to presenting. A phobia concerning presenting might have started when a child had been forced to stand in front of their school class, to be humiliated or bullied by the teacher and/or students. Or they might have seen this happen to other people and decided to 'keep their head below the parapet' or 'be thought a fool, rather than open their mouth and prove it'. Whatever the cause, the memory provokes fear, and not only is the person uncomfortable, to say the least, but their career can be impeded.

Tips for handling phobic people

Tricky, this. Richard Bandler devised what is known as the Fast Phobia Cure (or Ten-Minute Phobia Cure), which literally 'cures' the phobia in a short period of time. But I don't suggest that you attempt it without proper training from an experienced NLP (neurolinguistic programming) practitioner. Here are some practical alternatives that have a good track record, especially if tried during a calm period and not when an imminent presentation is looming.

What exactly might happen?

Often it is said that we fear the fear more than the event, and so this questioning approach avoids the fear and goes into the consequences, not the causes. It's best explained by an example, where F is the facilitator and P is the person whose fear you are about to dispel. The key rules for the Facilitator are as follows:

■ Keep P talking *about* things, not feeling them. It is essential to adopt a brisk, journalist-type voice, rather than using a soothing, caring, tell-me-how-awful-it-is tone of voice.

■ Ensure that P is talking about past events that were uncomfortable in the *past* tense, and future events in the *future* tense.

■ Choose a time and a place that's relaxed and comfortable, so that they can experience calmness, maybe for the first time, when thinking of how things will be in future.

EXAMPLE

P: I'm terrified of speaking in public.
F: So, you have been (note the past tense) terrified of speaking in public? What exactly were you terrified might or would happen?

(Allow P plenty of time to think. And if they start getting upset, briskly remind them that they are fact-finding here, and to sit up straight or stand up straight while doing so – as it's almost impossible to 'make oneself feel bad' while bolt upright. Try it – try sitting or standing bolt upright and saying, 'I feel depressed'; it's not at all convincing!)

P: I guess I'm terrified that someone might ask me a question I can't answer...?

F: So, you have been terrified that someone might ask you a question you couldn't answer. If that happened, what exactly might happen next? (And again allow plenty of time for P to consider this. It's highly likely that they've never thought seriously about it, having been terrified at the mere thought of it.)

P: I suppose I could just say 'I don't have the answer to that at the moment. I'll let you know?'

F: Good. And if you said 'I don't have the answer to that at the moment, I'll let you know?' – what exactly might happen next?

P: (Thinks a bit, then laughs...) I guess they'll just say 'OK' and I'll carry on!

F: And if you just carry on, what exactly might happen next? (Smile!)

P: It's OK, I think we're done, now!

This is based on many real-life cases. The turning point is when P smiles or laughs as they see how the situation probably would be handled, instead of their worst fear. In any case, it might be worth reinforcing this new-found realism with a few more situations – for example: 'So, tell me again how exactly you'd handle a situation where...?'

Worst fears

Another way of dealing with phobias practically is to put the person in front of an audience of three or four people who all are briefed to do what the person fears most – which might sound horrendous, but in practice it really isn't! Why not? Because:

■ the presenter is told that they can pause for thought at any time just by hitting the 'pause button'; or

- they can ask the audience for ideas about how they can be handled; and
- importantly, the audience can give feedback on what exactly worked for them and what might work even better.

This workshop technique works really well in groups of three or four because each person can take turns as the presenter. And let's face it, in reality most people know how to stand up and present. The problems they have faced are in not knowing how to address their fears, which have acted as barriers to putting into practice what they know perfectly well how to do.

36

Plodders

*who may also be Infuriatingly Slow, Tedious and
Tortoises (vs Hares)*

What ticks us off

They take *forever* to do even the simplest things. Why can't
they get a move on? Everyone else finished long ago but we're
still hanging around waiting for them. Grrr!

How it can happen

Let's be honest, some people are at the 'ultra-fast' end of the
spectrum, while others are at the 'ultra-slow' end. (We of
course are in just the perfect place, aren't we?!) And that's
something we have to accept. Different people's brains and
bodies go at different speeds and we can't change that. What
causes us to be infuriated, however, is when we compare – even
unwittingly – the slower performers with whatever our picture
is of the ideal performer. As it is said, we can only be disappointed if we first have expectations, so we need to have a real-
istic *range* of expectations. Not just 'fast'.

✓ **TIP**

Tips for handling plodders

The Plodder might well also be The Thorough, The Reliable, The Dependable, The Accurate, The Keeper-of-Promises, and The Steadying Influence. What strengths can we get them to play to, and can we praise them for?

Be precise

When I worked in advertising, the so-called plodders attracted much scorn, and a major target (see also the chapter on Impatient People) was the dispatch department. People would shriek hysterically about undelivered letters or packages that had been specified for delivery as 'ASAP' or 'As Soon As Possible' or 'Immediately'.

But if we stop and think about it, 'ASAP' is an unrealistic expectation since it is totally imprecise – 'soon' for you might not be soon enough for me. So we need to give precise deadlines. For example, 'we need this to arrive by X o'clock – at reception or the dispatch department or their home or their desk' – and then we can check that this is practical and affordable. At least we could then relax until X o'clock, instead of checking constantly whether it had arrived or not.

And that's exactly how we can establish deadlines with slower-working people, and indeed faster-working people. We can get *them* to plan how exactly they're going to do the task, and by when, and then commit to achieving that.

I'd *much* prefer a so-called plodder who can be relied upon to deliver on time, time after time, than someone who may be fast but who can only be relied upon as being unreliable.

Scientists

Many people with a scientific/mathematical background have been trained to 'show their workings', ie how exactly they've arrived at their conclusions or recommendations. In this way their thought processes can be checked by other scientists/ mathematicians in order to ensure that they've not only got the 'right' answer, but that they got to it in the 'right' way. That's why planes don't (often) crash and why nuclear power stations are (generally) safe.

But my goodness, these people can write hugely plodding documents and have unbearably plodding conversations without – seemingly – ever getting to the point. And that's the point – we now live in a headline society where we want to know the bottom line upfront, as it were. So we don't need long-winded displays of how people ploddingly (or meticulously in their terms) reached their conclusions. We just want a set of crisp recommendations. And we'll ask for explanations if we need to.

So, scientists who are moved into management (and I've met very few who actually chose to make this move) may well need loads of training and coaching and support, as they learn the crisp language of writing 'no more than one side of paper please' and trade in their piles of paragraphs for bite-size bullet points.

Don't let them get down

It's easy to think of Plodders as Downers. It's tempting to disrespect their pace instead of respecting their professionalism. They can get isolated and withdrawn. All that's needed occasionally is to choose a time when we're feeling a bit more relaxed and go and have a chat with them. Of course we don't need to expect a sudden full-blown friendship, just a more human and tolerant encounter. Simply by meeting them halfway, as it were.

37

Princesses and princes

*who may also be Daydreamers, Deluded, Precious,
Preeners, Spoiled or probably all of these rolled
into one*

What ticks us off

We're not talking about real-life royalty here: we're referring to
people who float around in a fantasy world of grooming and
glamour, and yet somehow seem – begrudgingly – to be holding
down a job. Actually, 'holding down' suggests much more
effort than they're capable of, except when planning their
extensive social life and catching up on other people's, when, as
opposed to doing the job they are paid to do, their energy and
enthusiasm are boundless. I've never actually met one who
wanted to work for a living, but they do get employed by other
princesses and princes, to keep their fantasies going, and to
keep real-life at bay.

How it can happen

Once upon a time, there was a spoiled little boy ('Who's
Mummy's little Prince, then?') and a spoiled little girl ('You're
Daddy's Princess!') who grew to believe that they were truly

special and that if they really wanted something enough and made enough fuss, then even 'No!' could be magically transformed into 'Yes!' For example, after just a medium-sized tantrum 'Of course you can have those trainers and whatever else Mummy's little Prince/Daddy's little Princess wants.' And they all lived indulgently ever after, well away from the real world of work, and objectives, and deliverables, and a fair day's pay for a fair day's work. Until they came to 'work' here. The End.

These people are, and will probably admit to being, high maintenance. They need to have the best (or what's thought to be best in their circles) and to be seen with the best. They physically ache if they want something badly. And so, not surprisingly, they're really hard to motivate and work with.

The only workplaces that truly amuse them are glossy, like reception areas – where they graciously receive their subjects between preening sessions – or the world of fashion. But they're largely there for the staff discounts and for the 'assistant manager' job titles (back to the fantasy world) and after a while they lose interest in what they can buy for themselves and their friends with their discount cards (magic wands?) and then they move on. Again.

Tips for handling princesses and princes

Absolutely fabulous

It does no harm to reassure princesses and princes on a frequent basis that they look absolutely fabulous or glamorous or whatever other words reflect their self-image, so long as we and the other mere mortals we work with know that we're doing this deliberately and for motivational reasons. After all, we try to motivate all individuals in the way that motivates them best, don't we, so why should we make exceptions?

You'll look great

Instead of just telling them what needs to be done, maybe we need to emphasize *how good they'll look* (since looking good is their prime concern) once the job is completed. We can also point out how we see that they're by far the best person for this task or role – again reinforcing how they see themselves.

Again this is just using their own state of mind to motivate them, which is no different from how we motivate anyone else, is it?

38

Repeaters

ie people who Keep Repeating Themselves

What ticks us off

Some people repeat what they've said several times. Or they say the same thing in very similar ways several times. Or they ask if they've mentioned it before. Or they just mention it again, without asking. And it can get irritating, puzzling and confusing. Like this.

How it can happen

Other than medical conditions such as amnesia or dementia, there are three common factors behind this tendency towards repetition.

First, the person has not *felt* heard – and so they go on repeating what they are telling you, whatever you have answered.

Second, they've not *noticed* that you've heard them, and so continue repeating themselves.

Third, they need to hear or see something more than once to feel convinced.

> ### 'Maybe next time'
>
> Most people from the United States that I've met have a 'convincer strategy' of One when it comes to restaurant recommendations. If they ask where they might go for a specific type of meal or ambience, they are highly likely to follow the recommendation.
>
> Most British people I've met, however, are likely to need to hear the same restaurant recommended at least twice (ie a 'convincer strategy' of Two or above) before they'll *feel* it's safe to try it.

Tips for handling repeaters

Eye them up

Sometimes the person may not have been looking at you, and if they were literally 'looking for' confirmation, they would not have seen it. So, whenever possible, look them in the eye when speaking in response to what they've said.

Add emphasis

In most cases, whether there was eye contact or not, you may simply need to say that you've heard them, but somewhat more emphatically than you had been doing, or more than once, to ensure that they've 'got the message'. For example, instead of just saying:

■ 'Uhuh' or
■ 'OK' or
■ 'Right',

you might need something like:

■ 'I hear you, and I'll consider it, thank you' or
■ 'OK, Mike, thanks for that, I appreciate your advice.'

This also replies in a repetitive fashion, modelling their own preference for repetition, and as it is literally 'speaking their language', it's more likely to be understood and heard.

Name them

Note that – as in the last example above – using someone's name can significantly help you 'get your message home', as there's no doubt who you are talking to. (Calling someone by name can connect with them at a deep level, not surprisingly, as it is their very identity that you are using.)

In a nutshell...

If it's clear to you that they are a bit trapped in their repetition, a useful focusing device for them is to say, or even interrupt with, something along the lines of 'I'm not very clear here: what exactly are you saying or asking?'

Check it out

You might also ask them why they are repeating themselves, when you have already responded. More often than not, people will say that they hadn't realized they were doing it, in which case you can ask what you can do in such situations to make it clearer for them.

It's not for you

Another very different pattern is where the person is 'just thinking aloud' and repeating themself to themself. I remember a friend telling me in no uncertain terms that he wasn't asking me for advice, thank you very much, and was neither asking for, nor interested in, my thoughts on the subject. I was a bit surprised, as he had been doing just that for about 10 minutes, I'd thought!

When I asked what part I *could* play in this conversation he just looked puzzled and said that he had been needing to think things through and I hadn't needed to respond at all. In fact, he'd have preferred it if I hadn't; I could read a book or watch TV if I wanted to.

So, subsequently, whenever I felt he was doing this, I'd interrupt gently and ask 'Am I going to need to say anything, or are you thinking aloud?' and he'd look almost surprised that I was still there!

39

Scatter-gun thinkers

who may also be Unfocused (actually Multi-focused) and Unpredictable and may Flit from Idea to Idea

What ticks us off

How infuriating it is when someone starts off with one idea, then goes off on a tangent, then another idea comes to mind (and out of mouth), and then another, and another – much like this sentence! It's hard to follow their train(s) of thought, to see where they're headed and, therefore, to keep up with them. And when we try to follow up on some of their thoughts, they've actually gone cold on them and are heading off in other directions! Phew, it's exhausting, and bewildering.

So we might dismiss them with 'Off they go again!' and leave them to themselves rather than involve them in meetings or conversations.

How it can happen

It's not as though any of the ideas are unappealing, but there's a confusion in the way that they're presented. Some people are simply thinking aloud. Others may get a strong gut feeling of 'Yes! That's a great idea!' to all their ideas, so they appear enthusiastic about almost everything. But when another one comes along, the previous one no longer seems appealing to them.

Their brain might also present them with a constant flow of new ideas and thoughts, and their editing faculties might not be able to keep up with their creative juices.

Tips for handling scatter-gun thinkers

This is a simple pattern to handle, whatever the causes.

Help them to focus

You simply need to stop their flow and bring them down to earth by asking them, for example, 'So what *exactly* are you saying or recommending?' or 'There seem to be lots of appealing ideas – can you prioritize them for us, please?'

Give them time to focus

It may be useful for them to realize that when they are in full flow, they will get stopped and sent away to focus – for example, 'You clearly have a lot of thoughts and we want to hear what they lead to, so can you let us have a clear recommendation in writing, please?' or 'This sounds potentially promising, so can you let us have a single recommendation either in a few minutes or in writing after the meeting?'

Not now

A quiet word, *not* when they are in full flow, could be extremely useful for pointing out this pattern to them, and explaining how off-putting it can be to others and, therefore, how potentially damaging it is to their reputation.

Maybe ask them if they recognize when they are doing this? Tell them that you're happy to support them in changing this pattern to a more meeting-friendly pattern, and to review progress with them. Offer them some tips that other people have found useful, and ask them to suggest other possible solutions – for example:

■ They could prepare bullet-point thoughts on paper first, and then edit them into those worth recommending that could enhance their personal and professional reputation, and those it's best to keep quiet about.

■ They could have in their mind's eye clear bullet points to talk from, before opening their mouth.

■ They could imagine putting themselves in the audience's shoes and listening to themselves making their points – and only say what they themselves would be keen to receive.

■ They could circulate a clear point of view before the meeting, and talk to that.

■ They should be encouraged to notice when they begin to flow creatively, and to remember that the meeting needs considered thought. At this point they should stop themselves by saying something like 'Actually, I'm going to stop talking right now and continue this brainstorming on paper rather than out loud.'

40

Selfish people

*who may also be Inconsiderate, Self-centred, Self-
obsessed*

What ticks us off

We don't get a look in! They don't think about anyone else. It's all 'me, me, me' for them. They ask how we are and then tell us all about themselves. They seem to think only about themselves. The world, after all, revolves around them, they seem to think.

How it can happen

It's simple: they think only about themselves! They see the world through their own eyes. And that's why we can sometimes feel manipulated, as they start by seeming to be interested in us, or considerate towards our position, but then lapse exclusively into their own perspective. They typically ask themselves 'What's right for *me*? What do *I* want or need or plan to do?' rather than a balanced (for example):

- 'What's right for me?' and
- 'What's right for you?' and
- 'What's right for the rest of the team?' and
- 'What's right for the organization?' and

- 'What's right in the short term?' and
- 'What's right in the long term?'

Tips for handling selfish people

Give them more time

When they've finished, point out that so far they've given a full account from their own perspective, and while you're naturally interested in that, you also need to know how they've considered it from other people's perspectives, and the organization's perspective, and whatever other perspectives they and you think are appropriate.

This may come as a surprise or shock to them – are there *really* any other perspectives?! So, offer them some time to think, and say that maybe they could drop you a note on the other factors to be considered, or you could meet up again later – to force them to think things through.

This approach *fully* respects their analysis from their own 'self-ish' perspective (after all, they probably have done it very expertly, after years of practice), and you will have acknowledged that, and then gone beyond that by asking specifically for more perspectives, and a well-rounded, not one-sided, point of view. (The hyphen in 'self-ish' means, to me at least, that I'm absolutely not judging them, just describing where they're coming from.)

Point them in the right directions

When briefing them, specify exactly which perspectives you want them to consider. After all, with a bit of prompting like this, it may well become a habit.

Warning

It is *not* a good idea to brand someone's entire *identity* in a negative and one-dimensional way, such as by telling them that they 'are' or 'are being' selfish.

It's much more useful to follow some of the above tips, and specify exactly what supplementary information you are looking for in the future (ie feed*forward*) rather than tell them what, in your opinion, they've done wrong in the past (ie feedback).

41

Show-offs

*who are Attention-seeking, Cocky, Extreme
Extraverts and Full of Themselves*

What ticks us off

Some people just cannot resist being the centre of attention, demanding attention, or getting the rest of us to stand to attention, irrespective of what we want to do, or what is appropriate to the situation. They physically crave attention, and if people are not paying attention to them, they can ramp up their attention-seeking behaviours (shouting, gesticulating, crying, etc) until they physically have to exit – dramatically, of course – by storming off, or fainting, for example, and often blaming others for not understanding, 'being stupid', 'giving them a headache', 'making them sick', etc.

How it can happen

This craving for attention may have many causes, eg a parent telling them that they should always strive for applause, or that they should always fill a silence, or that they will become invisible and unimportant if they don't get themselves noticed.

What's more interesting is that show-offs are often so busy getting noticed that they don't notice the effect they are having on the rest of us. We may avoid them, glaze over, not pay attention, or try to get away as quickly as possible. But they don't seem to notice. They only seem to notice applause, or being told how wonderful/clever, etc they are. Until they need to seek another dose of attention. It's exhausting for us and exhausting for them.

'I know, I know, I know'

I knew someone once who just couldn't shut up. Everything he said was essentially 'Look at how clever I am!', 'Tell me how smart I am!', and he'd repeat things over and over again until he got the response he craved.

Anyway, one day his most senior client – actually, his only remaining client – called him into a meeting and said 'Listen, I need to tell you something. I'm not happy…' – 'Oh yes, I'm really sorry about that', interrupted our friend. 'It was out of my control because we couldn't quite…'

'JUST a minute', continued the client. 'I'm not talking about that, I'm unhappy about…' 'Ah, right', interrupted our friend again. 'That really wasn't our fault this time because…'

'JUST hold it there!' interrupted the client again. 'What I'm trying to say is that I'm firing you, not just because of all these mistakes you've been making, but mainly – and don't interrupt me again, please – because I don't think you've ever let me finish a single sentence! I don't feel heard, listened to, or that you value what I have to say.' And with that, he walked out, leaving our friend somewhat surprised, but telling us how the client wasn't serious (he was, though) and how he, our friend, would save the day (he didn't, though).

Tips for handling show-offs

Pander to their need (apparently!)

The only way to get show-offs' attention is to give them what they need: praise. So, 'That's a great idea!' or 'Wonderful – that will be just what's needed!' or similar (and don't forget the '!') will normally stem their flow. (Note, though, that short praise, eg 'Perfect!' or 'Great!', may not be effusive enough for them.)

Then – and here's the bit *you* need, having given them the bit that *they* need – add what you need to say, eg 'But that idea is more about you than about our client's needs' or 'But I'd rather have something more thought through, please.'

And then, in a quiet moment, or in a regular supervision or appraisal meeting, address the pattern. For example, you could say 'We know you are smart, [their name], but we're getting tired of you trying to prove it all the time, and you don't seem to have noticed that people are getting reluctant to come into meetings with you, or ask your advice. Rest assured that your contribution is valued, but not when you ram it down our throats, because that's how it can feel. From now on, please consider your input, as we'd rather have your considered input than have to exclude you from meetings.' (And be prepared for them to look utterly astonished – because they've been too busy performing to notice – and to ask you for examples of this behaviour: have ready at least three recent instances to talk about.)

This direct approach may seem harsh, but nothing else you've tried has broken the pattern, has it? And in any case, being perfectly straight with someone is often the best approach. Tell them what they need to hear, fairly and squarely, and almost certainly you'll be thanked for your honesty, though maybe not immediately!

They'll have lots of food for thought. And you might want to ensure that they have a performance coach (who could well be their line manager) to help them to work this through and to modulate their approach to everyone's satisfaction.

Point it out

If you catch them doing this attention-seeking behaviour again, just try speaking their name to attract their attention, and then raising an eyebrow, or putting a finger to your lips, to signify that they're 'off' again. If they don't take the hint, take them aside, then or later, and explain what they were doing, again, and point out the specific abreactions from others present that they hadn't seemed to notice or to act upon.

Stressed people

*who may also be Anxious, Fretful, Pressured, Tense
and/or Worried*

What ticks us off

Some people are too stressed, they may say, to handle more
work, or different work, or perhaps any work. What used to be
a 'nervous breakdown' is now called a 'stress breakdown', and
stress is a major cause of absenteeism and sickness.

How it can happen

People under stress often have a sense of being the victim in
their scenario. Their sense is that they are affected by outside
causes – rather than *being a cause* themselves. And in many
cases this may be true, of course, as many people may have
work or family or medical or social situations that are not what
they themselves would have chosen.

But frequently they have exaggerated their situation with a
great big worst-case picture in their mind's eye of what might
happen, has happened or might happen again, and they can't
see passed it. And naturally anyone 'faced' with a big,
unpleasant picture like this is going to feel anywhere on a spectrum between intimidated and terrified, and naturally the
effects of thinking in this way can be to 'make' someone
worried 'sick' or to feel 'under' pressure, or 'stressed out'.

Tips for handling stressed people

At cause, not effect

Personally, I tend to avoid asking the person what they need to help them, as this can reinforce their feeling or perception of being helpless. (And in any case, if they knew what they truly needed, they'd have done something about it!)

First, I prefer to depersonalize it initially – for example: 'What exactly needs to happen for this situation to improve?' (Often they'll answer after taking some time to think, but then add that they don't see how this could ever be possible. Reassure them that you'll get to the *how* later, but suggest they concentrate on the *what* first.) Then, once they are clear about what needs to happen, I ask them to think about which of these whats they themselves could fix and which they'd need someone else to fix.

Only then is it timely to ask *how* exactly they might go about what they might do, and what exactly they need to do to get others involved. In this way, they are totally in charge of the plan – at cause, not at effect – and feeling as empowered as they truly can be, not as a victim.

Taking them literally

Many of the descriptions of how people perceive their situation suggest a direction. For example, they say they

- are 'under' pressure,
- are stressed 'out', or
- are unable to see a way 'forward', or
- are 'at the end of' their tether, or
- can't put 'up' with it, or
- feel put 'upon', or
- can't 'face' what's coming 'up', or
- feel that things are 'against' them, or
- feel that they are 'up against' a brick wall, or

■ can't go 'on', or
■ can't see 'beyond' tomorrow.

It's a common pattern, where people literally can't see an 'end' to it all. (And, interestingly, once they can see a light at the 'end' of the tunnel, they often can manage to summon up the resources to 'get through' it on their own.)

In most cases I would take them very literally. For example, if someone said they were 'under' pressure, I might ask what exactly would be needed to take the pressure 'off' them. Or a person saying they are 'up against' a brick wall might be asked how they might get 'over' it or 'around' it, or whatever other directions appeal to them. Even a person who says they can't go 'on' might be asked what they'd like to go on to, or even 'off' to. Using their own metaphors can help to unlock the *what* that would be preferable for them.

The big picture

If they have a big, scary vision of what they don't want to happen, you could invite them to put that as a small black-and-white still photo into a picture frame and invite them to see another dozen identical but empty picture frames alongside it.

If that was the *worst* that could happen, invite them to stretch their imagination to what could be even worse and put that into frame number 2. Then invite them to stretch their imagination even further and put an even worse still possibility into frame 3! (Sometimes I'll deliberately joke with them that if they had been imagining the worst, they must have a pathetic imagination, and surely they could come up with something worse than that! The reason for this is to put their worst fear into a different context – with 'even worse' possibilities – and to have them smile along with this process, to move them away from being stressed out 'by' it, and able to smile 'about' it.)

Then I'll get them to imagine in frame 4 what might happen that could be positive for them. And another positive one in frame 5. And – let's imagine you can do whatever you want to – well, go ahead and put those into the next few frames.

I'll remind them that it's their imagination and they can do whatever they want with it. (And we'll not worry for the moment about *how* any of these might be achieved.)

Then I'll ask them to attach a title to each of the picture frames (so that they have a way of describing them and so I don't need to ask them what's in each one) and to tell me the percentage probability of that picture happening for real. One hundred per cent is a dead cert that it'll happen, and 0 per cent is a dead cert that it'll never happen.

In this way they are:

1. generating other choices for themselves;
2. reviewing each one calmly (as it is contained by its frame, rather than being a sprawling 'inevitable' terror); and
3. reducing their stress by seeing them clearly and objectively (as each one has a considered percentage probability attached to it, rather than massive emotions).

And, finally, we can discuss which ones appeal to them that they might like to sleep on, before thinking about *how* they might happen for real.

43

Unassertive people

who may also seem too Compliant, Malleable,
Subservient or Weak

What ticks us off

There are people who don't stand their ground, or who can be persuaded easily against their better judgement, and so often end up overloaded, resentful towards others and disappointed in themselves – for example: 'I really can't stay late tonight... I've got something else I promised to do... I don't want to let them down... (pause)... well, I suppose I could rearrange it... well, OK then, I'll suppose I'll do it and stay late again.'

How it can happen

Unassertiveness is often, at heart, multi-assertiveness! Unassertive people change the destination of their assertion from, as above, 'I can't' to 'I could' to 'I can'. And, whatever the unassertive behaviour is, the person is often saying very assertively to themselves, 'Here I go again – why can't I hold my ground?!'

This is due, quite simply, to a lack of full stops.

Tips for handling unassertive people

Assertiveness is not the same as aggression. We can be perfectly assertive while being 'as nice as pie' or, better still, 'normal'.

What we say can be said assertively. *How* we say it can be firm and gentle. Here are some tried and tested ways of doing it that you might encourage the unassertive person to adopt.

Practise full stops

If the person had simply said 'I really can't stay late tonight' and then let the full stop be felt, that would have worked. (How do we let a full stop be felt? Follow it with a stonkingly good silence, while making eye contact from time to time.) This basically says 'I've said all I've got to say on this particular subject, so it's over to you, sunshine.' (I find adding the 'sunshine' helps to cement my resolve, but it's best said silently!)

If the silence seems embarrassingly long – that's good, because you have nothing else to say on this particular subject, remember? If you feel helpful, you could offer alternatives that genuinely are acceptable to you – for example: 'I really can't stay late tonight full stop. How about tomorrow night full stop? Or first thing in the morning?'

Change the subject

If the silence lasts over 15 seconds or so, let them off the hook by introducing a new subject – for example: 'Was there anything else?' or 'Fancy a coffee while I'm getting one?' so they're clear that you're still communicating with them, but there's no more to say on That Subject.

Keep it short and simple

Remember, the less you say, the fewer opportunities you're giving the other person to weaken you.

'Copy this'

Xerox once did a study of the excuses that worked best for secretaries to jump to the front of the copying queue. They tried 'My boss is more senior than your boss' and 'This is really urgent' and 'I'll get into trouble if I'm late with this.' But each of these is open to challenge – for example: 'Well, my boss needs it for her boss!' or 'Well, mine's really urgent as well!' or 'Well, you should have done it sooner!' The excuse that worked best, because there was less room to argue, was simply 'I need this copied now.'

'Hold your ground'

A designer, Gary, had produced some ideas for his client. The cost had previously been agreed at £2,700. The client liked the ideas, agreed to use them, and then said, 'But I'll give you only £1,500 for them.'

Gary calmly asserted, with clear full stops, that 'This took three days. I charge £900 per day. A total of £2,700.' The client blustered 'Come on, Gary, let's do a deal. £1,500. Cash if you like?'

Calmly again, Gary said, 'But we agreed £2,700 because it took three days and I charge £900 per day, so that's a total of £2,700.' Silence. The client did some more blustering, trying everything he could think of, including 'Well, I could get someone else to do it for £1,500.'

Gary stuck to his guns. Kept it short and simple. 'If you want these designs, they'll cost you £2,700. That's three days' work. At £900 per day.'

And it worked. The client shook his hand and told him he drove a hard bargain, whereas Gary just said (later, to me) that he had neither driven nor bargained; he had just stood his ground, knowing that he would either get the £2,700 that they had agreed, or would walk away with the designs and send the client an invoice anyway, since he'd sensibly got a purchase order in advance!

44

Unenthusiastic people

who may also be low on Ambition, 'Drive', Excitement, Inspiration, Motivation, Optimism or Passion

What ticks us off

Some people have enthusiasm, ambition, energy, focus, determination, passion and so on and on and on. If at first they don't succeed, they can indeed be very trying – as they'll do anything to satisfy their ambition and fuel the enthusiasm that drives them. Others, however, just seem to lack 'get up and go', and this apparent lack of enthusiasm can seem infectious and irritating, like a 'dampener' on other people's moods, like a 'wet blanket'.

How it can happen

There are potentially three patterns here:

Visualizing

Enthusiastic people are usually brilliant at visualizing big, bright, colourful pictures – often with sounds and smells – that are so real to them that they actually feel part of them.

No wonder that, with such compelling images, they have such compelling ambition. Other people, myself included, find it almost impossible to 'see' things in our mind's eye. At best there's a greyish cloud. And because there's less of an exciting picture for us to see, we're less excited, less enthusiastic and often less ambitious. Who yearns for a greyish cloud?!

'Do happy'

I was leading a project and in one particular meeting we seemed to be getting nowhere. One of my colleagues suddenly asked me to stand up and 'Do Happy'. I asked what on earth she meant! She said that she wanted to know what I looked like when I was really happy with a decision.

I stood up and, without moving more than my lips, said 'That's good' in a fairly flat, factual tone of voice. 'Good. Now do *really* happy', she said.

I stood up again and – standing pretty much stock still, apart from my lips, said again 'That's good' in the same flat, factual tone of voice. 'Very good. Now do so happy you couldn't be any happier!' she said.

Yes, you've guessed it; in the same flat, factual tone of voice, I said 'That's very good.' My colleagues were delighted: 'We were concerned that even though you said you were happy with our decisions, we didn't think you truly seemed happy, but now we know that you don't wave your arms around with happiness, or jump up and down, we need to modify our expectations and look for more subtle responses from you. We'd been confusing your subtle responses with a lack of enthusiasm.'

This was the first time I'd ever been 'calibrated' by colleagues, who wanted to ensure that we all understood how we responded, and how not to jump to inaccurate conclusions.

Do/don't motivations

Some people are motivated by what they do want (eg 'When I get enough money in the bank I'm going to get myself that car

I've always wanted'), whereas others are motivated by what they don't want (eg 'I don't want to do without a car and the one I have isn't running very well, so I suppose I'd better get some money together to get another one'). And, not surprisingly, those who are motivated by what they do want will inevitably have more energy for their tasks than those who are motivated by what they don't want. And that is why those in this latter group are often thought of as unenthusiastic, unambitious, miserable or even negative as a result.

Big picture versus detail

'Big picture' people get excited by their very first impression of a situation, and can easily overlook potential traps in the(ir) excitement. 'Detail people' take more time to consider the minutiae, and build up to an opinion detail by detail.

Imagine how infuriating it is, therefore, for someone who is at the extreme on all three patterns (ie very visual, with a very motivating 'want' and quickly seduced by a big picture) to be confronted with someone who is not visually imaginative, is more motivated by what they don't want, and takes time to consider the details. 'Hey, I've got this great idea for X – we can do A, B and C' can get the 'wet blanket' flopping onto the idea with an enthusiasm-dampening 'Yes, but how will we get the resources?' or 'But don't you remember it didn't work when we tried it back in 1990?'

Tips for handling unenthusiastic people

What have I missed?

If you are blessed with clear and motivating vision, remember that 'wet blankets' were born like that and are 'wired' like that! They are not deliberately 'miserable' or 'negative'; they just may not be wired to be able to see bright, exciting pictures, and may therefore come over as dull and unenthusiastic. Try welcoming their natural instinct to see how you might trip up, before you do so. Utilize their natural talents and ask them 'So, what are the pitfalls I've overlooked? What else might go wrong?'

Don't expect lots of energy and excitement that they don't naturally have in such situations. They may never show much enthusiasm or say that something is a 'great' idea – their minds don't work like that – but they might well agree to the proposition that 'If we dealt with all the potential pitfalls, then you'd have no objection to the idea?' That's the closest you'll get (ie a calm and genuine lack of objections) to enthusiastic agreement.

You might also recognize that, if their brain doesn't give them bright pictures to excite them, they might respond better to something like 'Why don't you drop me a note with your considered thoughts?' or 'Let me know later what I've missed, in my enthusiasm.'

No but-ter

Encourage the unenthusiastic person to banish the judgemental 'Yes, but…' from their vocabulary. Ask them to try something useful like 'That sounds really interesting/exciting.' (Because it does, to the other person or people.) 'Tell us more about it/how exactly it's going to work/how it's going to benefit us.' (And, in any case, since a picture is worth a thousand words, everyone else needs to have this picture described in much more detail before it can truly be considered.) Or 'I can see how that could work, and to ensure it does, there are three or four areas I'd like to think about.'

Emphasize a little

If they are naturally low in enthusiasm, and bearing in mind how I was calibrated (see 'Do Happy' earlier in the chapter), you might encourage them to try, in a calm, factual voice, adding a little emphasis and then a long pause after a full stop, to let the meaning sink in. For example: 'I am really happy with this.' (Long Pause.) Note that if the emphasis and enthusiasm are over-exaggerated, they will feel false to others too. Reassure them that a little emphasis from them will be received like a wild scream of delight from enthusiasts.

45

Unfulfilled people

*who may also be considered Failures, Inadequate,
Sad, Underachievers or Unsatisfied*

What ticks us off

These people can lack 'sparkle' – in their eyes, their voice, their walk, their work, even in their very being it seems. Something important is missing, and they know it, and people around them can usually sense it as well. Even if – or especially if – they try to cover it up with excessive forced cheerfulness.

How it can happen

Some people don't know what they want to do, and have had little sense of achievement, therefore. After all, if you know you don't have a destination in mind, thinking about setting off on a journey will seem pretty pointless.

Others may have known exactly what they wanted to do, but were prevented from doing it, either by other people or by their own abilities or by 'circumstances'.

Generally, however, they can feel less than whole as a result, and often express their feelings in terms of their entire identity – for example: 'I am a failure' or 'I'm no good' or 'I don't deserve any better' or 'I'm not worth it, in any case.'

✓ **TIP**

Tips for handling unfulfilled people

What you do is not who you are

One key approach is to stop people summing up (or summing down in these cases) their whole identity in this way, by separating their skills from their identity. This is a major step for many people, who have been thinking that because, for example, they did something badly, they therefore are 'bad'. And once this thought is in place, they will look for other instances of their 'being' bad, to confirm their belief. Indeed, people often have become so convinced that they 'are', for example, bad or useless that it can be a shock for them to realize that they do have some good things going for them.

So, you might need to be prepared to sit quietly with them, over the short term at least, while these realizations sink in. Here are some possible ways to begin:

- ■ 'I understand and can see that you feel completely useless, but you've always had a skill for doing X – better than anyone else I know, actually. And you're being very articulate right now about how you're feeling, so you clearly have some highly developed emotional intelligence skills and communication skills, even though you may not have recognized them as such. So, I'm wondering what other skills you might have overlooked? What else are you good at, or enjoy doing?'
- ■ 'You say that you're a complete waste of space, but I've chosen to continue employing you, because you're excellent at X and Y – and in fact no one else here comes close to your skill at Z. So, (twinkle in eyes) what *other* skills have you been overlooking?! And by the way, your kids seem to love and respect you very much, which also suggests that you've got pretty good parenting skills. So what others have you got?'

Follow your dream – but how?

Asking someone 'What do you really want to do?' is a big step, and so be aware that some people might be scared to admit what they really want, as they fear that they'll not be able to keep control of their wishes once they've admitted to them – whether to themselves or to another person. But it can cause real physical and mental illness if we continue to repress what we know 'deep down', and it will 'come out' eventually.

So yes, by acknowledging what they really want and then pursuing it, they may end up changing their current job, relationship, 'position in society', or whatever, but they will be gaining the freedom to pursue whatever truly, truly motivates them and satisfies them.

The very thought of this can naturally be terrifying and can bring even more feelings of inadequacy, because they recognize that they 'can't even do what they know they should do'. And so the key here is to separate the *what* from the *how*. I've noticed time and time again that most people fail to achieve what they want to achieve because they are concerned – rightly so – about how they will be able to achieve it, how they'll get the resources, the permission, etc. But when invited to forget about the *how* for the moment and concentrate on *what* they want, their immense liberation is palpable. I've never met anyone who, in a couple of hours maximum (with some facilitation, naturally, as it's often hard to see your own wood for the trees in these situations) has not been able to access what they truly want and to be motivated and excited and relieved by it. And they're in no rush whatsoever to answer the '*how* am I going to do it' question – the *what* is such a compelling proposition that they're willing to take some time thinking of different ways of achieving *what* they want.

Remember that 'success' is having a fixed *what* but variable *hows*. (The fixed *what* provides the real motivation. The variable *hows* enable us to try whatever we can, to achieve what we want. And remember also that 'If at first you don't succeed, *don't try it again* – it didn't work the first time! Try something *different*!')

But I don't know what I want

Many people would love to go for what they want, if only they knew what they wanted. This is very common, as very few people have a clear vision of what they see themselves doing. These suggestions may help, probably in combination rather than singly:

■ Realistically, they should be prepared to spend at least months on this as it would have been decided years ago if it were quick and easy to do.
■ Instead of their getting nowhere by trying to decide what they *do* want, get them to focus on what they *don't* want, and proceed by a process of elimination.
■ Find out what exactly, at a macro level, is the purpose of what they are looking for – for example, it might be paid work to *earn money*, or voluntary work to get out of the home and *fill time*.
■ Have them:
   1. develop a list of what they enjoy doing (work and pleasure together), eg outdoor walking and painting walls, and then
   2. write down the skills they have that enable them to do this, eg an understanding of nature, a patient and steady hand, and a critical eye for detail, and then
   3. think of where these skills might lead to in terms of paid work, voluntary work or whatever they are looking for. Then the person could:
      – Visit a recommended career counsellor (try asking for contacts at a local library, school or college).
      – Do research by following their instincts and networking: get them to think of who they know whose work seems appealing, or who seem to enjoy what they do, and then ask them about it, visit their workplace and read up about it.
      – Look through 'job wanted' advertisements in local papers and cut out three different types: those that look or feel interesting, those that seem appalling and

those that they are not sure about. Then be curious about what the advertisements in each of these three piles have in common: this will inform them about what *in principle* at a macro level interests them, appals them or intrigues them a little.

- Get a friend or friends to help with each of these tasks: it's much nicer and much more productive for them to be able to talk through their thoughts and have someone else ask them (non-judgemental) questions for them to consider.
- Be aware that this is likely to be a lengthy, step-by-step process, and that that is just normal.

But it's too late to get it

When someone knows what they really want (eg to be a champion sprinter), they might naturally feel disappointed (eg at age 80) that this seems unachievable. So, let's dig below the surface to find and then satisfy the WIIFM (What's In It For *Me*?).

You could do this by asking them, say, 'So, what would that do for you, being a champion sprinter?' and – if they are given time to ponder, and think what else it would do for them – the *real* reasons will emerge. For example, they may never have felt they could win something. Or they've always loved the feeling of speed.

So now you can explore other *hows* to achieve the feeling of winning (maybe you could explore different types of computer games?, card games?, arm wrestling?) or the feeling of speed (how about medically suitable and age-appropriate cycling, roller coasters or speedboats?).

Another example might be someone who had always wanted to be a medical doctor but who now feels it's too late to spend several years studying. You could again ask them, for example, 'So, what would being a doctor have done for you? What would that have given you?' and – again if they are given time to ponder, and think what else it would do for them – the real reasons will emerge. For example: 'I had a sick brother/sister and always wanted to help sick people' might lead to working in a doctor's office, or hospital, or hospice, and/or as a volunteer attached to one of these places, without their needing to restrict themselves to the first job they had thought of.

46

Unmotivated people

who may Do the Minimum, Need Telling Every Single Thing to Do, and also be Clock-watchers, Demotivated, Disengaged, Uninterested, Incurious, Lethargic, Reluctant, Slow, Timeservers, Uninvolvable or Unwilling

What ticks us off

It's really hard to get some people interested in work. And getting them interested is a necessary step towards getting them motivated to work – which, in turn, is necessary to get them engaged with their work. In desperation we may snap 'Don't you care about this?!', to which the neutral but honest response will be 'No. Not really.'

Irritatingly, they may well be motivated by something or someone else outside work, but at the end of the day it's down to us to make the motivation happen in the workplace.

And yes, we might be able to stimulate a spark occasionally, but it can seem to be up to us to keep their fire going, whereas truly motivated people are able to keep it going by themselves.

How it can happen

Incuriosity

Some people lack curiosity about themselves. (It was said that President Ronald Reagan lacked introspection because he was incurious about himself.) Some people lack curiosity about people around them, situations they are in, or indeed about life in general. And, not surprisingly, some people lack curiosity about their work, or the outcome of their work, or the use to which their work may be put. Maybe they have been told, at some time, to keep themselves to themselves ('Curiosity killed the cat!', they may have been warned).

Perhaps they had expressed an interest in the past but had had their spark extinguished by, for example, 'Just get on with your work and leave the thinking to me' or 'Don't go getting ideas above your station.'

Maybe there are too many other things going on in their life, and since they are just keeping their head above water, taking on one more thing might just be too much for them.

In a nutshell, no matter what the reasons are, they may just feel 'safer' keeping themselves to themselves, holding their tongue, keeping their head below the parapet, not playing with fire, and following the many other pieces of 'good advice' that they might have been given (and which may have been highly appropriate in a specific situation, but have been generalized out of all recognition).

Tip for handling incurious people

How on earth can we make it safe for people to get motivated? And to develop an inquiring mind, a hunger for learning, and their own agenda? Simply telling people that we want them to chuck away the habits of a lifetime, throw caution to the wind and risk opening their mind again might be *far* too risky an idea for them. They might think we're deliberately setting them up only to knock them down again. They may fear that they'll be blamed.

Do as I do

The very best approach, as in most things, is not to tell them what to do but to show them, as a role model. In a team, you can ask open questions such as 'So, what on earth do we think might be going on here?' and ensure that every possibility is valued, not rubbished or yes-butted. And it's essential not to force them to give opinions if they don't have any or don't yet feel safe to voice them. Let them gradually take away from the meetings the realization that you are genuinely not operating a 'blame' culture that could catch them out. Picking on the quiet people in a meeting is often recommended to ensure that everyone has their say, but in my experience it can frighten them further back into their shell and remind them why it's not safe for them to get involved, or put themselves on the line. It's often better to follow up with them individually after the meeting, and quietly develop their sense of involvement.

Twin tasks

In case the person has any fear of being 'exposed' in larger groups, pair them up with someone who's moderately curious, but not the most excited person you can find! Set them tasks that will stimulate the curiosity and interest of both members of the pair. Let the person feel safe, modelling curiosity from and with someone moderate, as a first step.

Be curious about their incuriosity

Bear in mind that sitting across a table or desk or in a meeting might not be as productive as something less confrontational. Maybe you could do it over a coffee or drink or lunch?

You could usefully model curiosity about their apparent lack of interest and motivation by finding out first of all what really does interest them (rather than by challenging them initially about their lack of interest!). Keep it open-ended. What else interests them? (Work or home, at this stage it makes no difference.) Then, when the time is right – and that may be at a later date – you can gently move forward with something like 'I enjoyed our chat and I've been wondering, from what you said, what you could think of that would improve your job for you? Both in terms of what you do, and in terms of how it's done?'

Be prepared for nothing

Some people will not actually have any interest in their job. None whatsoever. Their interest might be in what it allows them *not* to do (eg it might enable them simply to get out of the house, away from caring for others, not having to think about 'things'). And, for a job that doesn't depend on enthusiasm, that might be just fine. In fact, it might be preferable, if the job is somewhat repetitive.

'No swapping, thank you'

I remember the first time I saw a team of people doing intricate but very tedious, repetitive tasks, or so I thought. Hour in, hour out. Day in, day out. You get the picture.

I naively asked why they didn't regularly swap them around with other teams doing other tedious, repetitive tasks. 'That's a good idea, Mike, if we want to decrease their productivity and make them unhappy, and leave!', I was told. 'Er... please explain?', I fumbled.

'What are they talking about?', I was asked, and until that point I hadn't really noticed their chatter. It was about children and boyfriends and girlfriends and TV programmes and the weekend and – well, everything but work. 'Exactly, Mike. They can do this job in their sleep. They're with their mates. They can sort out where to go tonight, what to do at the weekend, shopping, local gossip – while their hands are automatically doing what's getting them paid. And you really want to disrupt all that?!'

What do you want...?

Often the simplest way of finding out what will motivate someone is to ask them. A tried and tested question begins with the four words 'What Do You Want...' followed by, for example, '... from your work?' or '... as a result of the promotion you're asking for?' or '... from this relationship?'

This question, when asked gently, is 'an invitation to consider'. It needs to be translated and asked of oneself (eg 'What *do* I want...') before it can be answered. It also presupposes that the person:

■ *does* want something;
■ *knows* what it is;
■ *can* tell you; and therefore
■ can acknowledge it and accept it for *themself.*

It can usefully be interchanged with 'So, what will that do for you?', which can dig beneath the surface to reveal *true* motivations.

EXAMPLE

Motivation

Q: So, what do you *want* from this job...?
A: I suppose, to be honest, just to get away from the house.
Q: OK, and getting away from the house, what does that *do* for you?
A: I guess it gives me a little feeling of independence?
Q: And this little feeling of independence – what does *that* do for you?
A: I suppose it makes me feel I have some value as a person? (Now you *could* get into deep and dangerous psychological territory here or – much more safely and productively – you could use this in a practical sense. For example...)
Q: I want to speak honestly here, if I may. We value (using their word) your work *enormously* in the following respects: X, Y and Z. Have I ever said that to you? Because we've been wanting to see how we can get you more involved/motivated for some while,

because we value your skills. So, let me ask you, what needs to happen for you to want to get more involved/motivated? And I'm happy for you to answer that now, or come back after you've thought about it; it's too important for us to rush.

The magic question

Incidentally, the question 'What needs to happen for you to want to...' is what I regard as The Magic Question as it invites someone to think about: 1) what really matters to them; and 2) how, practically, to achieve it.

And it's useful in many different types of situations – for example: 'What needs to happen for you to want to retract your notice and stay working here?' or 'What needs to happen for you and Mike to get on together?', or even to ask oneself, for example, 'What needs to happen for me to feel motivated about my work?'

Reframing

Reframing literally means putting a picture in different types of frame until you find the effect you want. For example, a black-and-white photo of a person in an ornate silver frame would have a different meaning to the same photo in a stark black frame – even though the picture is unchanged.

I *always* need to find an angle on something in order for me to feel truly interested in it and motivated by it.

'Boom!'

I was briefing someone on a workshop we were planning, and explained that at some point we would break into syndicate groups. I then told him, as an aside, that I hated the word 'syndicates', as it sounded so cold and clinical to me. 'Really?!', he exclaimed. 'I've always thought of Chicago in the thirties with all the syndicates battling each other for supremacy!' And ever since then, I've *loved* the word 'syndicates'.

So how can you help someone to reframe a job or a task to be able to get interested in it or motivated by it? Maybe you could hold a simple brainstorming session offering 'think of it this way' or 'think of it that way' ideas? Maybe you could think of another way of doing the task?, the benefits to the end user?, the benefits to the organization?

Or you could, again, ask a variation on The Magic Question, namely 'What would motivate you to want to do this?'

On the other hand...

By stimulating someone's motivation, curiosity or interest, you might indeed awaken their hunger for learning, self-improvement and progress. And as long as you can continue to fuel their flames – with learning and development and opportunities – that's great. But please be aware that they might outgrow what you can offer them, and be prepared for this.

47

Unrealistic people

who may be Overpromising Others and Kidding Themselves

What ticks us off

There's nothing worse than when someone makes a claim or a promise that you're pretty sure they can't deliver, except maybe – despite your querying it and receiving their assurances – when they actually fail to deliver.

How it can happen

Some people are so very, very, very keen to please that they'll promise anything. Often it's a throwback to school, where they were expected to second-guess the 'right' answer that the teacher was looking for. (This pattern in schools is rapidly changing, thank goodness.)

Frequently it's because they've been told that they should always say 'yes', no matter what the situation. Or that the customer is always right. Or that it's their job to say 'yes' first and then worry about how to do it later. Or that it's weak to admit that they can't do something, or don't know something.

None of these makes sense, of course, but they are habits that, once ingrained, become hard to break. (And the person *knows*, as they sound too sure and look too certain that, inside, they are feeling very anxious about the situation!)

Sometimes, also, it's simply a lack of knowledge or the ability to plan ahead that causes unrealistic promises to be made, but there's generally at least one of the underlying beliefs mentioned above that underpin it.

Tips for handling unrealistic people

Ask how, exactly

If you have even the *slightest* suspicion about someone's ability to deliver, ask them to let you have confirmation in writing of exactly *how* they'll be doing what you've asked.

This will unfortunately mean putting to one side your excitement at the fact that they've apparently promised you a fantastic deal/bargain/delivery date, but it's enough that you've caught *them* being unrealistic without you getting caught in the same trap.

Think twice

If you have found someone overpromising for a period of time, it might be that they are simply responding to flattery. It's easy to do. Maybe they'd been asked to do something and had been told that 'only you' could possibly achieve this. Then what often happens is that:

■ they feel proud/happy to be asked if they would like to do X, and then
■ they say 'yes'.

Where this 'yes' really comes from is:

■ yes, thank you for thinking of me;
■ yes, thank you for asking me;
■ yes, thank you for your flattery (to get me to say 'yes'!).

What they might do, however, is to say honestly, 'Yes, I'd love to' or 'How nice of you to think of me!' or whatever they truly feel. And then add a small voice of reason with, for example, 'I'll just have to check my diary/ask my boss/partner and see if I can practically do it. I'll ring you in the morning.' And then they should go away and ask themselves:

- If someone else were doing this, would I be in the least bit interested in going to see/hear/work with them?
- How is this going to benefit me, if at all? (Financially? Educationally? Reputation? Warm glow inside?)
- Can I physically fit it in?
- Do I really *want* to?

And then, if it's important, they should sleep on it. And talk to other people about it, if in doubt. Or talk to the person who invited them, if they have any questions. And then they can realistically accept, or honestly say they would have loved to do it (which is always true) but don't have the space in their diary for it. Phew.

48

Untrusting people

who may also be Cautious, Cynical, Hard to Convince, Sceptical or Suspicious

What ticks us off

Whatever someone may ask them or say to untrusting people, their first response is to sceptically raise an eyebrow, ask 'Re-a-lly...?' and give every sign that the other person is from another planet full of beings not to be trusted or believed. And even if they don't do any of these precise things, it will certainly *feel* as if they had!

Trust and respect are of course very desirable but not always instantly achievable. People fall into two camps. One camp assumes that other people cannot be instantly trusted or respected, and that trust and respect must be earned over time, with repeated experience. (It may be a general belief about all people, or may be linked, on the basis of previous experiences or prejudices, to a specific trait such as 'shifty eyes' or 'blonde hair'.)

Those in the other camp, however, are more 'trusting' and willing to give others the benefit of the doubt. They assume that other people are trustworthy and deserving of respect unless they prove otherwise.

Naturally, a lot depends on how much is at stake. A chance meeting or conversation with someone you are unlikely to meet again can be enormous fun even if you know they are exaggerating wildly, as they are of no consequence to you. On the other hand, similar traits in a friend's partner may make you very concerned for the consequences for your friend.

Mistrust and disrespect are barriers that are hard to penetrate or overcome, and in an organization (or a family) they can seriously obstruct the essential process of open communication.

How it can happen

Trust is not actually a feeling, like 'warm', 'cold', 'tense' or 'relaxed'. It is first and foremost a thought or a belief, one that typically is created by realizing that there are shared values of, for example, honesty, transparency and decency, which in turn leads to a comfortable, relaxed feeling – for example: 'I feel I can trust her completely.'

Even in a criminal or hostile context, trust could still be engendered by very opposite values to those just listed, eg dishonesty, subterfuge and indecency, provided they were shared by all those involved. So, if values are shared, no matter how contrary to our own they might be, then trust can exist between those who share them.

'Thanks but no thanks'

I remember a boss of mine whose judgement I generally respected but whose actions I didn't initially trust. Why? Because his motivations and values were for the greater good of all the organization's clients, I later realized, whereas mine were focused, naturally, on my own clients.

As I gradually realized that we had different, but complementary, agendas, I found it easier to see the bigger picture from his perspective, as well as my own point of view. The specific occasion when I realized this was when I'd prepared a thorough discussion paper and recommendations for him, and he replied, 'Thanks. I agree with everything you've said and recommended.

But I'm not going to implement it, and here are the three reasons why. But I thank you for all your work.'

Did I feel rejected or angry? Not in the least. His thanks were for my input, and they were genuine. His reasons for not implementing it were clearly explained to me and made complete sense from his perspective. Respect.

Over there

Next, there are cultural differences. I've noticed that people from the United States, for example, are much more trusting of something or someone new than people from the United Kingdom are. If someone from the United States asks for a recommendation for a restaurant, they're likely to trust you and try that restaurant. In the United Kingdom, however, they're likely not to trust it until a few people have recommended the same place and they've grown used to the idea that it might be worth a try. (Unless, that is, the recommender has an impeccable track record.) It seems that the older a culture is, the deeper the trust and respect are for institutions and conventions – not surprisingly, since they've been around for longer. Therefore, the more conventional people and their ideas are, the more likely they are to be trusted (as in 'tried and trusted').

In newer cultures, newer ideas are more likely to be considered seriously, and strangers are more likely to be given the benefit of the doubt.

Recovery

Talking of track records, the expression 'once bitten, twice shy' comes to mind. It might be easy to *forgive* someone who caused you to lose trust or respect, but it's not possible to *forget*, and once respect and trust are lost, they are almost impossible to regain. The sense of loss of trust or respect can be very profound, and can be at the level of the person's very sense of self – for example: '*I* was let down' or 'He/she made *me* look small.'

✓ TIP

Tips for handling untrusting people

Don't take (or give) lack of trust personally

If the lack of trust or respect is taken or given personally (rather than behaviourally), it can feel very wounding and it can be almost impossible to repair – for example: 'You are a liar' or 'I don't trust you' or 'Who believes what you say, any more?'

Move the conversation away from the personal onto the behavioural – for example: 'What did I say or do (that caused the problem for you)?' or 'Let's discuss the issue, not the people, please. Your issue with what was said or done is... what, exactly?'

Avoid making personally wounding statements such as 'You are a liar' or 'I don't trust you.' Stick to specific facts rather than generalized character assassinations – for example: 'What you promised did not happen' or 'Your organization has a track record of delivering late to us.' (And then keep quiet. Allow the other person to digest what you've said, and then respond. If the discomfort is too much, then, after a pause, you might want to add something like 'Why not think it over or discuss it, and let me have your considered response?')

The ball is in their court... not yours

Trust and respect need to be earned back, if they have been broken. If you were at cause, you might ask, for example, 'What exactly do I need to do for you to trust/respect what I say or do, again?' and allow time for the person to consider this.

They might come up with something specific such as 'Deliver on time the next three or four times, or advise me well in advance if there's a problem.' Or you might get a blanket rejection such as 'I can never trust anything about you again'. In this case you might try something like, for example, 'I understand that's how you feel right now. But if there were something specific that I could do or say, what might that be?'

'Three steps to trust'

I was leading a training session, and during one of the breaks one of my colleagues came up to me and said that they'd been speaking to one of the quieter participants who'd said something that I might be interested in: 'Because I feel that Mike trusts me...' (long pause and intake of breath), 'I feel that I can trust Mike' (even longer pause and intake of breath) 'and therefore...' (pause) 'I can begin to trust myself.'

I've come across this three-way structure on many subsequent occasions. Trust builds step by step for people who've had good reason to be suspicious, or who've been let down. Until it begins to flow, backwards and forwards, it can't settle where it's needed most. After all, some people have had horrendous things said and done to them and have had their very good instincts drummed out of them (and if you can't trust your own instincts, what can you trust?).

For me, the most horrendous ways are those that masquerade as 'good advice' or 'for your own good' – for example: 'You should always do as you're told' or 'People should respect their elders and betters.' These bits of 'good advice' may have been relevant in a specific situation at a specific point in time, but do not work as generalizations.

After all – or actually, *before* all – if we can't trust or respect our 'self', what on earth can we trust or respect? That's why this three-step strategy is a useful way of modelling, and therefore of building, trust and respect.

49

U-turners

who may also be Backtrackers or Mind-changers

What ticks us off

They'd agreed to a deadline, now they say they didn't. They recommended X and now they recommend Y. They wanted pizza, and now they want pasta. They never stick to what they said. We never know where we are with them.

How it can happen

By changing what they originally said or meant, they create confusion and distrust. This leaves us uncertain of where we stand and, interestingly, it leaves the U-turner just as uncomfortable.

The key is that these people – if we think back – were never confident in what they said in the first place, but we probably overlooked that at the time as we were happy to have a decision or agreement to rush off with.

For many of us, this harks back to our schooldays when the name of the game was to come up with the 'right' answer as quickly as possible. Many of us still play this game even though the 'game' is so totally different at work, and the largely self-imposed pressure to come up with a quick 'answer' causes absolute havoc in organizations, and we can include families and friends as organizations too.

What's needed in organizations, and indeed in life, is to come up with smart questions, not quick answers. Quick answers may be fine for very simple questions like What's the capital of Turkey? We either know it's Istanbul, or we know we don't know, so either way we know where we stand. In life, however, we deal with more complex situations which are often new to us. We first of all need to understand the nature of the situation, and the implications of any decisions that we might make, all of which takes time. And if there is more than one person involved, then a shared understanding needs to be reached, which takes even more time. It *needs* to take even more time. (And yes, you're right, it's Ankara, not Istanbul: see how easy it is to feel satisfied with a 'quick' answer, even if it's not a useful one!)

So, consider our poor U-turners who get pressured into reaching premature conclusions. When they make their U-turns they are not really changing their mind – they'd never truly made up their mind in the first place.

And – this may sound strange, but please bear with me – one sub-group of U-turners may simply be trying to please other people by giving the answer that they think we want to hear. They, I'm told, are Cancerians, astrologically speaking. (See case study 'Cancerians' on page 198 and skip to the last two paragraphs on page 199 if you want the succinct version!)

✓ **TIP**

Tips for handling U-turners

Give them time

It's so seductive and energizing to go round a room and check that everyone is in agreement so that 'we can move on, yes?' It's tidy, it's done and dusted, and the chairperson gets a sense of achievement. But many people get a sense of unease that will grow and grow until they 'feel uneasy' about the decision and can then analyse why this is, and eventually articulate it.

Maybe we should never be expected to make complex decisions in meetings (I know of many organizations that have been doing this for years!). We should be sent away, asked to think through the issues and implications, do whatever research we feel is necessary and then put our name to a recommended course of action or inaction by a certain deadline. And everyone should be clear that 'I don't know what to recommend yet' is a perfectly responsible position to hold.

Consider this

A practical approach would be for us to let the U-turner know that we want a considered answer, not a snap answer. (An even more practical approach would be to engender a culture where everyone understands the sense of this.)

'Cancerians'

I wanted to go to the Market Research Society conference. I asked my boss who said 'Fine. Just write a paper, get it accepted, and off you go.' I explained that I wanted to go as a delegate. He just repeated 'Write a paper, get it accepted and off you go.'

I'll show him, I thought. I started wondering how on earth could I, a mere trainee, get a paper accepted? What subject would stand out amongst other papers and also interest me enough to write it? I decided that novelty-value was the best approach, as rejection was not a result that I wanted. I thought about market research. Typically a survey is analysed for similarities and differences between different age groups, genders, socio-economic groups, etc. And that's when the answer struck me. Astrology has been around for about 5,000 years. There are 12 different star signs. It would be really easy to ask people which sign they are, and then to look for similarities and differences between the 12 groups.

I found a massive annual survey of social attitudes (and surely if there were any differences between the star signs they would manifest themselves in social attitudes?) which would be perfect for my purposes and which I could 'piggy-back' onto. So I rang the managing director of the survey company to explain what I wanted. She got very excited and explained that her chairman was really into astrology. He wouldn't hire any staff without referring to their astrological chart. And, as it happened, they were just finalizing this year's survey and could get the results to me just in time. I hurriedly wrote a proposal for the conference committee and I got an enthusiastic acceptance. So I could go to the (conference) ball!

Fast forward a few weeks. The results came through and I wrote 12 paragraphs, each one a pen-portrait of one of the star signs. Very, very dull. This would definitely ruin my reputation even before I'd made one. So, in my normal fashion, I told everyone I could about my problem. How could I make this interesting rather than a tedious list of, well, 12 tedious lists? And then, as luck would have it, someone said 'Aha. Do you know Pat Smith (not his real name)? He's a statistician, he lectures on market research, and he's a well-known astrologer!'

So I went to see Pat Smith, who read through my paper, smiled occasionally, nodded a lot, and burst out laughing derisively a couple of times. He explained that he didn't believe I was inexperienced in astrology as 'Ten of the 12 are spot on. Even the way you've written them is characteristic of their characteristics. One of them makes no sense at all – Gemini – but then they are so complex that it's hard for anyone to make sense of where they're coming from. And one of them is complete rubbish – Cancerians.'

Before I could get into a discussion with him, his doorbell rang and he let in a woman who was dressed like a whole troupe of stage gypsies. There were no introductions and he simply thrust my paper into her hands and said 'Tell me what you make of that, then?' She read through it and smiled and nodded and exploded in derisory laughter in exactly the same places as Pat had. 'Absolutely spot on,' she said, 'except for Gemini and Cancer of course.' And she looked me sternly in the eye. 'You should never interview Cancerians, young man, because – dear people that they are – they will always give you the answers that they think you want to hear!'

And I've found, if I 'innocently' turn the conversation to star signs, many u-turners were born under the sign of Cancer...

50

Workaholics

What ticks us off

At times, nothing about workaholics bugs us, as they can be extremely useful to have around when there's a lot of work to be done and they are willing and able to do it! But that's only sensible short-term. If it becomes the normal way of working, then the person will be more likely to 'run themselves into the ground' and possibly affect their health and/or family life in the process. Moreover, it can affect the rest of a team, who might feel that they too should be staying late or working weekends, or whatever.

How it can happen

There are many reasons for working significantly longer hours or days than other people. Some people enjoy their work and are simply very willing. Some feel that 'the harder the worker, the better the person'. Some have a home life they'd rather stay away from. Some get work dumped upon them and are unable to stand up, or speak up, for themselves. Some are unable to cope in normal working hours, and spend more time, therefore, to cope or, in some cases, to continue not coping. Some people competitively try to notch up more hours than others, or to seem as though they do. For instance, I once had a colleague who had spare jackets that he used to leave on hangers and on the back of his chair to make it seem as though he was in the office when other people arrived and departed!

Tips for handling workaholics

Whatever the cause(s), the 'cure' is the same. The intention is to establish a healthy (ie not stressed) pattern of working for the individual, for their team and for their work–life balance.

Inevitably, everyone has a different set of criteria. For example, some people have more stamina, while others have more outside demands on their time, but the solutions are widely applicable.

Facts

First, establish what exactly the situation is – for example: 'I notice that you've been working later than other people, getting in earlier and coming in at weekends, but I'm not aware that your workload has changed significantly. Can we talk about it, please? What exactly is going on?'

Second, stick to your guns. Don't accept 'Everything's fine, thanks', as you need to ascertain exactly what is going on. This pattern can, as we've seen, have serious consequences for the individual, the team and the family.

Third, understand exactly what your organization's written policy is on work–life balance (you do have one, don't you?), so that you can talk with the person about:

■ your personal concerns, and
■ their own situation, in the context of
■ the written policy.

In this way, you can negotiate towards an acceptable solution for all concerned – for example: 'I'm happy for this to continue for a couple more weeks so long as your partner's away and you've not sorted out some evening and weekend activities for yourself. We'll review it on (specific date), yes?' or 'Leave it to me to speak to X about doing their own work and not expecting you to do it' or 'So we're agreed that you'll leave on time, without worrying that other people are still working?' or 'Your job description needs looking at, given these changed situations. Will you let me have a proposal? Or shall I do it?'

'Budapest'

I was working with a group of fresh-from-college trainees. There was clearly something bothering them, and eventually one of them asked very timidly, 'Mike, if you've finished your work, is it OK to go home?' I asked each of them to look straight at me, not at each other, and to raise a finger in the air if they agreed that:

1. It's important to do your job well.
2. It's important to have a social and home life.
3. When you've done your job for the morning/afternoon/day/week, it's time for your social and home time, and it's OK to leave work.

Everyone gingerly put up a finger to agree with every one of these, not surprisingly. At number 3, I asked them all to look around very gently and see if anyone else had a finger up. The fingers all stayed up but the mouths all dropped open. Each one was genuinely surprised that everyone was of the same opinion as they were.

So, having determined that everyone was agreed about the principle of going home when the work was genuinely finished, the next step was to decide how to put it into practice. I asked how they had handled it in the past. They replied that they found things to do for as long as they could, because other people were still apparently working. And then, having plucked up courage, they crept out as silently and, they hoped, as unnoticeably as they could. And – this was the accompaniment to *all* their actions – they inevitably felt very guilty.

Therein lay the solution. What was the opposite of 'feeling guilty', I asked. The agreed answer was 'feeling proud', and so they brainstormed some practical feel-good exit lines (in Hungarian, of course, translated here for the rest of us), eg:

- 'I'm finished – have a good evening, everyone!'
- 'I'm off, out to dinner. Good night!'
- 'I'm off for lunch now, see you at 2!'

And even just:

- 'Bye, everyone!'

'What's wrong with Joe?'

In a very competitive team, Joe (let's call him) had always been the first into the car park in the morning and the last to leave at night. Gradually the other team members started following his example and also started coming in early and leaving late. After a few weeks of this, everyone was really tired, work and family life were suffering, and the quality of the work was deteriorating.

How to break this pattern? A consultant was given this project by Joe's boss, along with a 'cover' project so that he could get to know the team in the meantime. He quickly realized that this pattern had spread to a café down the road, where the team would assemble even *before* work started! And so he too arrived there as soon as the café opened, and soon another team member arrived, startled to see the consultant there, of course. When asked what he was doing there, the consultant said that he was worried about Joe. Was there something wrong with him that he couldn't get his work done on time, did he know?' He just wanted to check with Joe's workmates before the boss had to take action.

The next morning, another of the team members was the first to arrive, and got the same message, and gradually the word got around that if you couldn't do your work on time, there could be something perceived to be wrong with you! Mission accomplished.

51

Yes people

*who appear to Agree with Everything and have
No Real Opinions of Their Own*

What ticks us off

It's hard to get an honest opinion from these people, which can leave us feeling very frustrated, because if we don't know where they stand, it's harder to know where *we* stand.

Their answer to most questions about what they think or want or prefer is along the lines of 'What do you think?' or 'Whatever you like' or 'I'll go along with the majority' or 'Anything you say/do/want/agree is OK by me.'

'No yes'

I remember working with a multinational team in Japan. My normally calm German client was yelling at my Japanese colleagues, 'I'm sick and tired of you agreeing with me all the time, whatever I say. I want you to challenge me more. I need you to question my thinking more robustly. I want you' (and by this time he was shrieking almost impossibly) 'to Stop Saying YES All The Time!!'

After a stunned silence, one of my Japanese colleagues, trying to be helpful as always, ignited a veritable volcano when he politely replied, 'Yes, Sir.'

How it can happen

There are many possible factors here:

- Some people have been told never to disagree with their 'elders and betters', and so they don't.
- Others might have been led to believe that their opinion 'doesn't count' or 'doesn't matter' or 'isn't worth a light', or that they should 'keep their head below the parapet'.
- Many believe that 'the customer is always right' and want to be seen to be acting on this all the time, even if it's to their own disadvantage or to their organization's detriment.
- And, on occasions, we can all be put on the spot if someone barks at us 'Yes? OK? Is that clear?' and we find ourselves replying, 'Yes' in a sort of daze. And when we come to our senses, we realize that we're in a bit of a mess here, having agreed with something we don't agree with.

Tips for handling yes people

Honesty is the best policy

They need to be honest. Not painfully or brutally honest, but simply honest. After all, if their mouth is saying 'yes' while their body language is saying 'no' or 'not sure', other people will be picking up these mixed messages.

The advice many people were given as a child to 'speak only when spoken to' or to 'agree with our elders and betters' might have been useful at the time, but it might not be appropriate in all current situations! They can better follow their own instincts and intellect now.

You could suggest, therefore, that they simply and honestly say what they feel – for instance: 'I'd like to say "yes" to be polite, but I'd rather give this some thought and get back to you.'

You could also suggest that they ask the other person for clarification on what exactly they are asking or expecting – for example: 'Are you looking for me to agree with you, or do you want an honest considered opinion, or what else are you needing from me?'

Look to yourself

Maybe we ourselves can take some responsibility, as we might well have been provoking the 'yes' answers – and in future we can get the answers we really need by changing how we invite them. For example, we may need to ask smarter questions than 'Yes? OK? Is that clear?', since most people who feel 'put on the spot' can find themselves blurting out the first thing that comes to mind – ie 'Yes' or 'OK' or 'That's clear' – while panicking inside!

We could ask, 'What's your honest opinion about this? or 'Can you consider this and let me know the pros and cons?'

We could look at the person saying 'yes' and check out their body language and eye contact, to ensure that it's a whole-hearted (ie whole-body) 'yes' rather than a forced or false one.

We could even ask them, in a quiet moment, how we could get them to be more open with their opinions, by inviting them to tell us what exactly *we've* been doing that's been inhibiting them.